SELF-CORRECTING
CORRECTING
LEARNING
MATERIALS
FOR THE CLASSROOM

Cecil D. Mercer
University of Florida

Ann R. Mercer
University of Florida

Deborah A. Bott
California State College—Bakersfield

Charles E. Merrill Publishing Company
A Bell & Howell Company
Columbus   Toronto   London   Sydney

Published by
Charles E. Merrill Publishing Co.
A Bell & Howell Company
Columbus, Ohio 43216

Production Editor: Molly Kyle
Cover Designer: Cathy Watterson

Library of Congress Catalog Card Number: 84-60007
International Standard Book Number: 0–675–20134–9
Printed in the United States of America
1 2 3 4 5 6 7 8 9 10—88 87 86 85 84

To our parents

Lois and Arden Mercer
G. Randolph Robertson and in memory of Eleanor Robertson
Mary Lu and Robert Bott

Contents

Preface

The importance of immediate corrective feedback is well-established in the teaching-learning paradigm. Since most teachers are responsible for teaching groups of students, the task of providing immediate corrective feedback to individual learners becomes very difficult. This book illustrates self-correcting learning materials for providing individualized feedback.

Self-correcting materials are easy to make and provide feedback without requiring the presence of the teacher or other instructional personnel. In our experiences with self-correcting materials over the past ten years, we have found these advantages:

Students enjoy immediate feedback.

Students do not practice mistakes during seatwork.

Self-correcting homework reduces frustration and promotes independence.

Students tend to learn better with immediate rather than delayed feedback.

Self-correcting activities promote on-task behavior.

Students become more independent during seatwork.

Self-correcting formats can be used in various subject areas.

This book features a variety of easily-used self-correcting formats applied across several content areas: math, language, reading, spelling, written expression, and other subjects. Skill hierarchies will help teachers in planning and monitoring pupil progress. Chapter 8 discusses commercial self-correcting materials, and chapter 9 discusses microcomputers and instructional applications that feature immediate corrective feedback.

This book is designed for preservice special and regular education methods, strategies, and techniques courses. At the inservice level, it is appropriate for make-it/take-it workshops, as a resource material, and in instructional resource centers. Parents will also find the book useful for creating home tutoring materials.

We hope the book will help teachers provide their students with successful and meaningful learning experiences. Finally, we would like to thank Vicki Knight, Molly Kyle, and the art staff at Merrill for their assistance in the publication of this book.

SELF-CORRECTING MATERIALS EXPLAINED

People need feedback to learn. Although many additional elements are required, feedback seems to be irreplaceable. Sometimes feedback is painful—the sensation of the head hitting the floor when learning to walk. Sometimes feedback is pleasurable—the wonderful tastes and compliments after cooking a good meal. People are always looking for feedback in conversations, at work, in sports, and in the mirror. Knowing the consequences of what we do is crucial.

Consider this situation: a student is working independently on a page of math that will be returned the next day with the mistakes circled. Although this type of feedback is typical, it is not optimal. The 24-hour time lapse between completing the paper and receiving feedback is too slow to be effective, the circles around the incorrect items do not reveal the correct answers, and the student is not instructed to use the feedback in practicing the correct response. In the classroom, feedback is best when it is immediate, when it models the desired behavior, and when it is followed by practice on what needs improvement.

When students work independently, teachers can provide quality feedback by using self-correcting materials. These specially designed materials allow the learner to make a response and then compare it immediately with a model. Self-correcting materials provide feedback without the need for a teacher's presence or for a grade. After completing an assignment, the student sees or hears the correct responses, becomes aware immediately of items not mastered, and has the opportunity to practice.

Experiences in teaching and research demonstrate the effectiveness of self-correcting materials in holding the learner's attention. If the required task is appropriate and the design of the materials is appealing, students like to work with them. The gamelike format allows students to compete with themselves or the task, rather than with their peers. Thus, motivation is a positive result of self-correcting materials.

In addition, when given the choice, students prefer private mistakes to public ones. Self-correcting materials allow students to commit mistakes without everyone's knowing. This factor is especially important for students with a history of academic failure. They do not lose status when they make errors with self-correcting materials; their mistakes are private.

Self-correcting materials also eliminate a common shortcoming of seatwork: practice in making errors. Through feedback from the material, the student can quickly see which items or tasks he has not yet mastered; he can make changes and try again.

If a teacher gives a student the answers, cheating is an obvious possibility. Cheating with a self-correcting material may be defined as looking at the answer before making a response. Many students may enjoy beating the system initially, since the answers are so accessible. However, if students are not following the proper directions, cheating can be handled. For example, when a clear relationship is made between tasks in the self-correcting material and a mastery exam, cheating becomes pointless. Students quickly realize that cheating does not help in the end.

Case Studies

Several case studies have been conducted at the University of Florida to examine the influence of self-correcting materials on learning. Figure 1.1 presents the results from three case studies conducted in an elementary school. Each child was pretested on a list of words. Words that the child had not mastered were identified and randomly assigned to a self-correcting intervention and a worksheet intervention. Thus, each child received instruction on words equated in difficulty under both self-correcting and worksheet conditions. Worksheets included a variety of common formats (such as blanks to be filled in and crossword puzzles) and the self-correcting materials included Poke Box, Answer Box, and Answer-on-Back Cards (see chapter 2 for descriptions of these self-correcting materials). Instruction occurred for 10 minutes daily over 20 days and with equivalent time spent on each material.

   Learner 1 was a fourth grade boy who attended a special education resource room for one period a day. He was identified as an emotionally handicapped student. The self-correcting and worksheet materials were used in the child's regular class during reading instruction. The results in Figure 1.1 indicate that he mastered (that is, could see words—say words at a rate of 75 or more correct per minute) 45 words using self-correcting materials and 15 words using worksheets.

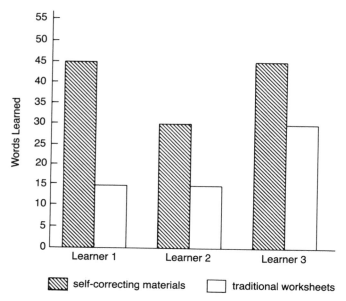

Figure 1.1. *Comparison of words learned using traditional worksheets and self-correcting materials.*

Learner 2 was a fourth grade girl who attended a special education resource room for one period a day. She was identified also as an emotionally handicapped student. The study was conducted in the learner's regular classroom during reading period. The results indicate that Learner 2 mastered 30 words using self-correcting materials and 15 words using worksheets.

Learner 3, a third grade girl also identified as an emotionally handicapped student, attended a special education resource room for one period a day. The study occurred in the learner's regular classroom during reading period. The results indicate that she mastered 45 words using self-correcting materials and 30 words using worksheets.

The results from these and other case studies suggest that self-correcting materials are effective in helping some students learn more quickly. Moreover, if these three learners' results were maintained for a semester, the number of words they learned could increase dramatically.

Design and Construction

Individual needs and learning styles should influence the design of self-correcting materials. This does not mean that each student requires a complete set of personalized self-correcting materials, but the teacher should be aware of the match between the student and the material. Commercial self-correcting materials are available, but often the teacher must design them.

Simple designs require less construction time and permit straightforward directions for use. Durable materials initially may be more expensive, but they are eventually more efficient in terms of cost and time than other materials. The self-correcting materials should fit on a desk top. If the student is required to write a response on a sheet of paper, the size of the paper must be considered in the dimensions of the material. These materials are generally not consumable; that is, marks are erasable or are made on a separate piece of paper.

Students may construct self-correcting materials, both for their own use and for use by others. Again, simple designs are an advantage. Student involvement in constructing the materials may increase motivation to work with them and could be presented as a reward activity that is both productive and fun.

Place in Instruction

Self-correcting materials may be used throughout the learning process. Initially, the teacher and student may use the material to assess how well the student can perform a task. Next, it is mandatory for the teacher to provide the necessary instruction for and demonstration of the skill by showing proper use of the self-correcting material prior to its practice by the student. Finally, a student may be required to demonstrate mastery of the task by performing it with the self-correcting material against a predetermined set of standards. Varying the formats of self-correcting materials and the manner in which they are used will help to maintain students' interest in the materials and in the skills to be learned. Materials that have different formats but address the same skill provide several different ways to practice a task and may make the difference between achievement and failure for some students. Providing a variety of materials that cover the same content also allows the student to have a choice as to which material to use for practice. Choice is a strong motivator which should be included in academic plans. Finally, exchanging self-correcting materials or putting some away for a time may make them seem novel when they reappear on the shelf.

Self-correcting materials may motivate students to practice outside the classroom as well by overcoming difficulties often associated with homework. For example, they assure that the student is not practicing incorrect responses, and parents may feel more comfortable when helping their child with homework if there is no pressure on them to provide the right answers. Second, since the materials are simple to construct, duplicates may be made for use at home, without fear of forgetting to take them back to school or ruining them.

Organization of Materials

Self-correcting materials may be organized according to the structure of the academic content used in any classroom. The materials themselves may be stored in file drawers or cabinets in a systematic way that corresponds to the academic hierarchy, skill level, or textbook used for instruction. A card file of available materials is useful when planning students' assignments.

Conclusion

The remainder of this book will present a total of 12 basic formats for self-correcting materials. Then, each format will be applied in a slightly different way for each major academic area. The formats are intended only as starting points for planning, making, and using self-correcting materials. Although the directions given are explicit, they are not intended to limit what form the material may take or what function it may serve. Scope and sequence skills lists for each academic area are included at the end of each chapter to provide the teacher with a hierarchical ordering of skills which can be taught and practiced via the use of self-correcting materials. In addition, selected commercial self-correcting materials are listed and self-correction in relation to computer software is discussed.

Self-correcting materials may deliver feedback in diverse ways limited only by the five senses and the designer's imagination. The challenge is to create a material that provides needed practice on a skill and understandable feedback. Once this is accomplished, the learner's time spent working independently on a skill can result in its mastery.

THE 12 BASIC FORMATS

Various feedback devices may be used to make self-correcting materials. We present the following 12 basic self-correcting formats: answer on back, cassette, colored acetate folder, flap, holes, light, matching, pockets, puzzles, strips in a folder, stylus, and windows. For each format, selected instructional pinpoints, feedback response, materials, construction, directions, and modifications are given. The teacher may adapt these formats to individualize instruction and present activities in any academic area. Selected examples of the use of each self-correcting format in math, reading, language, spelling, written expression, and other subjects are presented in chapters 3 through 8.

Answer on Back

A problem is presented on one side of a stimulus card, and the answer is placed on the other side. This format is especially adaptable for older students needing practice with any type of fact or definition.

Selected Instructional Pinpoints

Any task may be used in which a problem has a single correct answer.

1 See clock face—write time in digits
2 See multisyllabic word—copy word and divide it into syllables
3 See name of state—say name of capital city

Feedback Response

The correct response is written on the reverse side of each stimulus card.

Materials

Index cards
Pen or marker that does not bleed through to reverse side of card

Construction

1 Write the problem or stimuli on one side of the card.
2 Write the answer on the reverse side of the card.

Directions

The student arranges the cards so that the stimulus side is face up. The response required may be written or verbal. After each response is made, it is checked with the answer on the reverse side of the card.

Modifications

An entire page of problems may provide the answers on the back, spaced to correspond with the learner's written responses on a separate piece of paper. Also, students may make their own sets of cards and work with them outside of class.

Cassette

Cassette recordings provide auditory stimuli and give directions to the student to make a response, usually written. After a pause for each response or group of responses, verbal feedback is given on the tape.

Selected Instructional Pinpoints

Any pinpoint requiring the student to listen to a problem or question and write or say a response may be selected.

1 Hear spelling word—write word
2 Hear "digit times digit"—write product
3 Hear definition—say biology term

Feedback Response

The student listens to the recording and hears the correct answer. A written or verbal response made previously is checked against the information given on the tape.

Materials

Blank cassette tapes
Cassette recorder
Headphones (optional)

Construction

1 Prepare the script for recording. Know exactly what will be said and include instructions about the material to which the learner will need to respond.
2 Find a quiet area for recording.
3 Insert the blank tape in the recorder and press *record*.
4 Speak clearly and allow pauses for the learner to make responses.

Directions

The student selects a tape, inserts it in the recorder, puts on the headphones, and plays the tape. Pauses are provided when the student is to make a response, or the tape may be stopped if more time is needed. Each response is checked against the answer given on the tape.

Modifications

The rate of presentation of stimuli may be changed to encourage increased proficiency. Also, for practice in oral reading and/or comprehension questions, a selection may be recorded and the student may be allowed to see and hear the text. For increased interest, allow students to make the tape recordings.

Colored Acetate Folder

A durable colored acetate folder may be used with many different activities by simply changing the specially prepared sheet that is placed inside the folder.

Selected Instructional Pinpoints

Any task requiring a written response will work well with this format.

1 See geometric figure—write name of figure
2 See description of character from a story—write character's name
3 See incomplete spelling word—write missing letters

Feedback Response

A worksheet with the stimuli written in dark ink and correct responses written with a yellow felt-tip marker is placed inside a colored acetate folder. The responses written in yellow cannot be seen through the colored folder. The learner writes his answers and then opens the folder to compare them with the correct responses.

Materials

Colored acetate folder (red conceals the yellow printing best)
Dark-colored pen
Yellow felt-tip marker
Grease pencil or acetate marker (optional)

Construction

1 Prepare a worksheet with the stimuli material written in a dark color.
2 Write the answers on the worksheet with a yellow felt-tip marker.
3 Insert the worksheet in the colored acetate folder.

Directions

The student receives a colored acetate folder with the appropriate worksheet placed inside. He writes responses either on a separate piece of paper or directly on the acetate with a grease pencil. The student checks his answers by removing the worksheet from the folder and comparing his responses with the answers written in yellow.

Modifications

Crossword puzzles may be used and completed in yellow pen. The teacher can develop these or take them from magazines, newspapers, or crossword puzzle books.

Flap

A flap may be made of any flexible material such as cloth, vinyl wallpaper, construction paper, or thin cardboard. When using the learning material, the student can bend the flap up or to the side to reveal the answer to the question or problem. The Answer Box[1] illustrates the use of one type of flap to provide feedback.

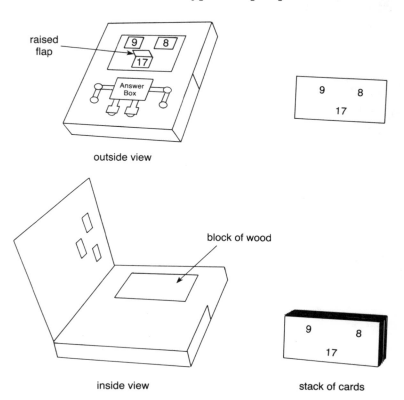

outside view

inside view

stack of cards

Selected Instructional Pinpoints

Any task requiring a brief oral or written response may be used with this format.

---

[1]From *Teaching Students with Learning Problems* by C. D. Mercer and A. R. Mercer. Columbus, Ohio: Charles E. Merrill, 1981, p. 90. Copyright 1981 by Bell & Howell Company, Reprinted by permission.

1 See math fact or problem—say answer
2 See math fact or problem—write answer
3 See contraction words—write contraction
4 See percentage problem—write answer

Feedback Response

A flap is placed over the mouth. When the flap is raised, the answer is revealed. Vinyl wallpaper is flexible and serves as a good flap.

Materials

Cardboard box (for example, cigar or school supply box)
3″ x 5″ index cards
Contact paper or lamination and paint
Small wooden block, approximately 3″ x 3½″

Construction

1 Cut out three squares in the lid of the box so they form two eyes and a mouth.
2 Cut a section out of the right side of the box so the index cards can be fed into the box from the side.
3 Paint the box inside and out.
4 Laminate a picture of a face on the box and place the eyes and the mouth over the squares.
5 Place a flexible flap over the mouth.
6 Prepare index cards with problems and answers so that the problem appears in the "eyes" and so that the flap over the mouth can be lifted to reveal the answer. For math problems, a grease (overhead projector) pencil can be used to write the math operation ($+$, $-$, $\times$, $\div$) in the space between the "eyes."

Directions

The student inserts a stack of selected cards into the Answer Box. Then the student responds (orally or by writing) to the problem presented in the two windows. He lifts the flap on the mouth to reveal the answer and check his response.

Modifications

The card formats can be varied to provide a variety of math problems and numerous reading tasks. These are some possible card formats:

___ at	16 4	20% $1.60
cat	4	32¢
Initial Consonants	Division	Percentage

Holes

Problems are written on one side of a card or sheet of paper, and a hole is punched beside or underneath each item. The answer to each problem appears on the back of the card and is written next to or under the corresponding hole.

Selected Instructional Pinpoints

This format works well with tasks requiring a brief answer such as a number or a single word.

1 See 4-digit numeral—write the numeral that is in the 10's place
2 See word—say its synonym from a vocabulary list
3 See uppercase letter—write corresponding lowercase letter

Feedback Response

After writing or saying his answer, the learner puts a pipe cleaner or pencil through the hole next to the problem. He then turns over the card and checks his response with the answer written next to the hole marked by his pencil.

Materials

Manila folder
Hole puncher
Gummed hole reinforcers

Construction

1 Write problems on the manila folder.
2 Punch a hole below or next to each problem, and reinforce each hole with a gummed hole reinforcer.
3 On the reverse side of the folder, write the answer to each problem next to its corresponding hole.

Directions

The student says or writes the answer to a problem and then pokes his pencil through the hole next to the problem. He then turns the folder over and checks his answer with the one appearing next to his pencil.

Modifications

The hole format may be used with multiple-choice questions. A hole is punched next to each choice and on the reverse side the correct-answer hole is circled in a color. Problems can be presented individually on index cards instead of folders so that the student sees only a single answer each time.

Light

A light may come on to provide feedback for correct responses. The Electric Learning Board[2] (p. 20) illustrates the use of this feedback device.

Selected Instructional Pinpoints

Any task in which the student selects the correct answer may be used. Also, tasks requiring more than one correct answer may work with this format.

1 See picture—select word
2 See math fact—select answer
3 See paragraph—select fact or facts
4 See word—select plural

Feedback Response

The student inserts the stylus in one of the holes to indicate his response. The light turns on to indicate a correct response.

Materials

Cigar box (wooden or cardboard)
#12 bare copper wire (single-strand)
#16 insulated wire (stranded)
Light bulb and socket
Battery
Plastic tape
¼" quarter-round wooden sticks
Epoxy glue
5" x 8" index cards (unlined)
Hole puncher

---

[2]From *Teaching Students with Learning Problems* by C. D. Mercer and A. R. Mercer. Columbus, Ohio: Charles E. Merrill, 1981, p. 94. Copyright 1981 by Bell & Howell Company. Reprinted by permission.

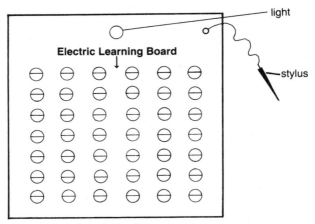

light

Electric Learning Board

stylus

Outside Top View

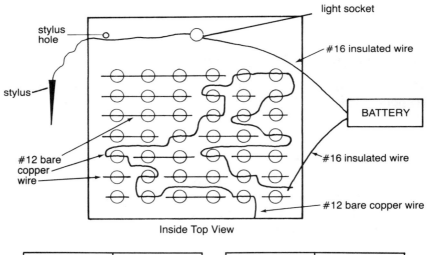

light socket

stylus hole

#16 insulated wire

stylus

BATTERY

#12 bare copper wire

#16 insulated wire

#12 bare copper wire

Inside Top View

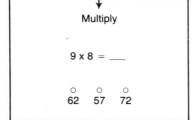

Multiply

$9 \times 8 =$ ___

62   57   72

Percentage

$21.00

$22.50

$48.00

30% off coupon

$45.00 price

new price
___

Stimulus Cards

Construction

1　Drill holes in the top of the box to cover the area of a 5″ x 8″ index card. Six holes across and seven rows down are adequate.

2　On the inside of the box, place the copper wire so that it passes under two holes on each row. Glue the wire. Connect this wire to one terminal of the battery. These are the correct-answer holes which will cause the light to turn on.

3　Glue the copper wires under the other holes. Be sure that none of the copper wires touches the live wire, so that the correct-answer holes cannot be determined. All the holes have copper wire passing under them, but only underneath *two* holes per row is copper wire that is hooked up to the battery.

4　Connect the second terminal of the battery to one terminal of the light socket.

5　Drill a hole in the top of the box to the right of the light socket. Make a stylus using #16 insulated wire with #12 bare copper wire at the point. Wire the second terminal of the light socket to the stylus.

6　On the outside top of the box, make a border for the 5″ x 8″ index cards so that they can be fitted over the holes properly. This may be done by gluing the ¼″ quarter-round sticks around the three sides of a 5″ x 8″ area. The bottom side is left open to slide the card into the space. Make an arrow on the box to indicate where the top center of the stimulus card should be when properly inserted on the Learning Board.

7　Make a key card with the correct-answer holes marked so that other cards may be made easily by fitting them over the key card.

8　Make stimulus cards that present a task and a multiple-choice answer format using holes in the cards. Place the hole for the correct response so that when the stylus is placed in it, the light turns on.

Directions

The student places a stimulus card on the Learning Board and inserts the stylus in the hole for his answer. If the choice is correct, the light turns on.

Modifications

Tasks that require more than one correct answer may be presented on the Learning Board. For example, the student may be instructed to locate six places in a paragraph where punctuation is needed. The light comes on to indicate each correct response. When there is more than one response for a stimulus card, the student should be instructed to make a certain number of answer choices.

Matching

Sets of cards are prepared with the problem or question on one card and the answer on another card. The back of the set of cards contains a match of some sort or a picture completion.

Selected Instructional Pinpoints

Any skill involving matching of two or more parts, question/answer, or sequencing is applicable.

1 See fraction—write equivalent percent
2 See letters—sequence alphabetically
3 See name of state—write abbreviation

Feedback Response

The back of the set of cards contains a match of some sort or a picture completion. When the student has responded to a problem, the cards are matched or placed in sequence and turned over. If the appropriate answer is chosen, objects, symbols, numbers, colors, or pictures will either match or fit together to complete a picture.

Materials

Cards of any size
Pictures from magazines or newspapers (optional)

Construction

1 Write questions and answers on separate cards.
2 On the reverse side of each question/answer card set, draw or paste matching objects, symbols, numbers, colors, or pictures.

Directions

The student arranges the cards so that the stimuli are face up. The cards are matched or sequenced and then turned over. The response is correct if the reverse sides match or form a picture.

Modifications

The student may be required to sort the cards initially by questions or one type of stimulus and then write a response. The cards are then matched and the reverse sides checked. For picture completions involving sequencing or matching more than two cards, the student may construct the sequence on a small piece of cardboard. When complete, a matching piece of cardboard is placed on top and both pieces are turned over. When the first cardboard piece is lifted, the picture should be constructed correctly. An additional modification involves the use of clips such as clothespins or paper clips to provide feedback by matching. For example, a piece of cardboard in the shape of a pizza is divided into segments with a task stimulus presented in each section. Responses are made by clipping clothespins on the edges of the segments. To check answers, the student turns over the board to see if the code on the pizza board matches the code on the clothespins (see the matching activity in chapter 5).

Pockets

Pockets may be attached to the learning material and used in one of two ways. The pocket may contain an answer key or it may be coded with some sort of symbol to match with stimulus cards when they are sorted properly.

Selected Instructional Pinpoints

Virtually any task requiring a response to a stimulus may be used with this format, providing that the required answer is consistent. Pockets are especially appropriate for pinpoints requiring categorizing.

1 See line—measure with a metric ruler to the nearest centimeter
2 See words on cards—categorize according to parts of speech
3 See photo of animal—sort according to animal family

Feedback Response

An answer key may be placed in the pocket or the outside of the pocket may display a symbol that corresponds with a symbol on the backs of the cards. When the cards are placed in the correct pocket, all symbols match.

Materials

Library card pockets, envelopes, or any type of paper, plastic, or fabric that can be used to form a pocket
Glue, tape, or staples
Worksheets, tagboard, or manila folders containing directions and stimuli materials
Answer key or category cards

Construction

1 Form a pocket and attach it to the worksheet or folder.

2 Insert the answer key, or for a sorting activity, prepare the cards and code the reverse side of each card with a symbol that matches that on the appropriate pocket.

Directions

The student responds to a stimulus as directed and then removes the answer key from the pocket to check for accuracy. For categorizing activities, cards are sorted face up. The learner places the cards in the appropriate pocket and then checks the reverse sides of the cards to see if the symbols match that on the pocket.

Modifications

Items to be categorized may be written on puzzle pieces so that when the sorting is completed, each pocket will contain pieces to complete a puzzle. Also, answer keys and worksheets may be cut from commercial materials and workbooks.

Puzzles

In this type of feedback, pieces of material fit together to indicate a match or correct choice. Puzzles may be simple pairs of pieces with a question or problem on one piece and the answer on its match. More complex puzzles may be made for activities requiring sequencing of several components. The sections will interlock only if they belong together. Beware of passive puzzles! Require the student to write or to demonstrate the academic response. Do not let the learner ignore the material's message by only matching pieces. Use the puzzle to get feedback only *after* another behavior has been completed.

Selected Instructional Pinpoints

Any skill that may be presented as a matching, question/answer, or sequencing activity is appropriate for puzzles.

1 See one digit plus one digit—write sum
2 See picture—match word
3 See definition—write prefix

Feedback Response

Sections of the puzzle fit together to reveal the correct match or sequence.

Materials

Stiff paper or cardboard for puzzle pieces
Scissors
Paper and pencil
Laminating film (optional)

Construction

1 Cut a whole shape for each individual puzzle.
2 Write or draw two or more parts of the activity on the shape.
3 Cut an irregular line or lines between the parts.

Directions

For a simple two-piece puzzle, the student sorts puzzle pieces into two piles—the questions and the answers. The student draws one piece from the questions pile and writes down the proper response on a piece of paper. He makes a row of the pieces left to right across the top of the desk in the order drawn. After all the questions have been answered, the student draws from the answer pieces and completes the puzzles. He then checks the corresponding puzzle pieces with the written responses that he made. For a sequencing puzzle, the student arranges the pieces in sequence and then checks to see if they fit together in that order.

Modifications

Materials such as balsa wood, felt, or stiff plastic may be used for puzzle pieces. Also, pieces may be reused when peel-off labels are used.

Strips in a Folder

Strips are cut in one side of a laminated manila folder. Worksheets containing problems and answers are inserted in the folder so that only the problem is presented. The student makes a response and then the worksheet is pulled upward to reveal the answers.

Selected Instructional Pinpoints

Math problems worked vertically are well-suited for this format. Any problem that can be written within the exposed area and its answer covered by the strip is appropriate.

1 See two numerals—write correct inequality symbol ($>$ or $<$)
2 See two words—write contraction
3 See name of month—write name of month that directly follows it

Feedback Response

The student writes responses on the laminated strip with a grease pencil and then moves the worksheet upward to reveal the correct answers.

Materials

Manila folder
Laminating film
Grease pencil
Scissors
Worksheets prepared with problems and answers in alternating rows

Construction

1 Open a manila folder and laminate the left half.
2 Cut strips out of the laminated side.
3 Prepare worksheets so that when they are inserted in the folder, the problems are visible and the answers are covered.

Directions

The student inserts the worksheet in the folder so that the answers are covered by the strips. He writes his answers with a grease pencil on the laminated strips directly under each problem. When the worksheet is completed, he moves the worksheet upward until the answers show in the cut-out spaces. The student checks his answers with those appearing directly above the strips.

Modifications

Strips may be cut out of a colored acetate folder and the answers should be written in yellow below the problems.

Stylus

Feedback may be provided by using a stylus with certain types of stimulus cards. The Poke Box[3] illustrates the use of a stylus.

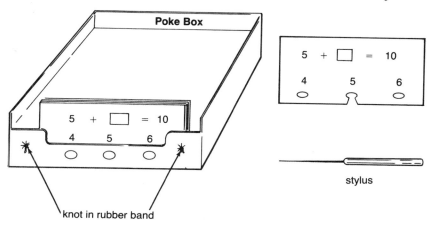

Selected Instructional Pinpoints

Any instructional pinpoint that features a multiple-choice answer format may be used with the Poke Box.

1 See math problem—choose answer
2 See math problem—write answer
3 See sentence—choose missing word
4 See paragraph—choose title

Feedback Response

The student inserts a stylus in one of the holes below his answer and pulls on the card to see if it comes out of the box. If the right hole is selected, the card is easily removed from the box since the area below the correct answer is cut out and offers no resistance to the stylus.

---

[3]From *Teaching Students with Learning Problems* by C. D. Mercer and A. R. Mercer. Columbus, Ohio: Charles E. Merrill, 1981, p. 92. Copyright 1981 by Bell & Howell Company. Reprinted by permission.

Materials

Cardboard or wooden box big enough to hold 3″ x 5″ or
  5″ x 8″ index cards
Large rubber band
Paint
Thin stick or poker
Index cards
Hole puncher
Gummed hole reinforcers

Construction

1 Cut the front end of the box so most of the
   index card is visible, but leave a horizontal
   strip at the bottom of the box about 1″ high.
2 Using a hole puncher or a drill, make three
   evenly spaced holes across the front of the box
   about ½″ from the bottom.
3 At each end of the front of the box, drill or
   punch a hole that extends beyond the dimensions of the index cards. Insert a broken rubber band from the inside of the box on both
   sides, and tie the ends in knots on the outside
   of the box. The rubber band holds the cards
   and pushes them to the front of the box.
4 Paint the box inside and out.
5 Make holes in the index cards so they line up
   with the holes in the box.
6 Cut out one answer slot on each card.
7 Attach the stylus to the box.
8 Prepare index cards with problems or questions on top and possible answers beneath.
   Line up the answers with the appropriate
   holes.
9 To prevent a student from tearing the card
   by pulling too hard on a wrong choice,
   strengthen the holes with gummed reinforcers.

Directions

The student says, writes, or chooses his answers. Then he pokes the stylus in the hole representing his answer. If the choice is correct, the problem card can be pulled up and out of the box and the next problem card is presented.

Modifications

The size of the box may vary so that large cards can be used. Some Poke Boxes feature 8″ x 11½″ cardboard cards. The large space provides room for short stories and multiple-choice comprehension questions. The teacher may put the problem or story on a separate worksheet and put the answer selections on the cards. A stylus may be used with other materials such as pockets made from manila folders or heavy felt.

Windows

Small windows may be cut in materials to provide feedback. The correct answer may appear in the window or, when two or more windows are used, the items in the windows can match to show a correct response. Spinning Wheels[4] illustrates the use of windows.

Selected Instructional Pinpoints

Any pinpoint can be selected in which a matched pair can be devised (i.e., problems on one wheel and the correct answers on another wheel).

1 See match problem—select answer
2 See picture—select word
3 See picture—select initial sound

Feedback Response

Windows provide feedback. When a correct match is obtained in the front windows, the objects, symbols, or numbers match in the back windows. Thus, to check an answer the student looks at the back windows.

Materials

Poster board
Brass fasteners
Small pictures or symbols
Scissors
Laminating film (optional)

Construction

1 Cut two rectangular pieces of poster board with matching dimensions.

---

[4]From *Teaching Students with Learning Problems* by C. D. Mercer and A. R. Mercer. Columbus, Ohio: Charles E. Merrill, 1981, p. 91. Copyright 1981 by Bell & Howell Company. Reprinted by permission.

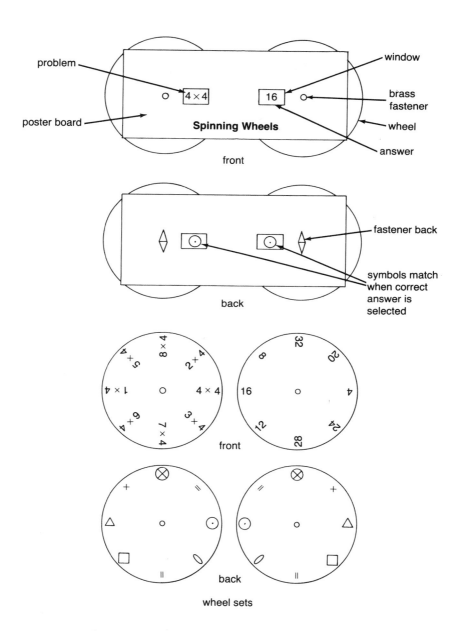

problem

window

brass fastener

poster board

wheel

answer

4 × 4   16

Spinning Wheels

front

fastener back

symbols match when correct answer is selected

back

4 × 4
4 × 8
5 + 4
2 + 4
1 × 4
4 × 4
6 + 4
3 + 4
7 × 4

16
32
8
20
4
12
24
28

front

back

wheel sets

2 Cut two windows on the same horizontal line in each piece. The windows should line up with each other when the pieces are placed together (back to back).

---

3 Decorate and laminate each piece, and make holes next to the windows for fasteners (see illustration).

4 From another piece of poster board, cut circles with dimensions that enable the outer 1″ ridge to be seen in the windows of the rectangular pieces of poster board when the center of the circle (or wheel) is lined up with the poster board hole.

5 Write, draw, or paste problems in one wheel and put answers on a corresponding wheel. Write, draw, or glue symbols, objects, or numbers on the back of each wheel set.

6 Place the wheel set between the rectangular pieces of poster board and fasten with brass fasteners.

Directions

The student selects a wheel set that presents the task that the teacher wants him to practice. He places the wheels between the two rectangular pieces, lines up the holes, and inserts the brass fasteners. The student then rotates the task wheel until a problem is presented in the window. Next the student rotates the other wheel and selects one of the answers that passes through the window. Once an answer is selected, the student flips the material over and checks to see if his answer is correct. A correct answer yields matching objects in the two windows on the back.

Modifications

Teachers can make many wheel sets and code them according to skill area. Wheels that are to be used together (a wheel set) should have matching codes on them. The tasks that can be placed on the wheels are almost limitless. The material can be varied to accommodate windows of different sizes.

3

MATH
MATERIALS

This chapter illustrates the use of self-correcting materials for teaching math skills. An arithmetic scope and sequence skills list at the end of this chapter illustrates some of the many skills and concepts for which self-correcting materials are helpful. The list includes addition, subtraction, multiplication, division, fractions, decimals, money, time, and measurement. Because these materials are useful in several areas, they enable the teacher to individualize seatwork and/or homework.

Answer on Back: Time

Pinpoint

See clock—write in numerals
See time in numerals—draw clock

Aim

To write the time shown on the clock and/or draw the clock face
with two or less errors

Feedback Device

The correct answer is written on the back of each stimulus card.

Materials

Index cards prepared with a clock face drawn on one side
and the corresponding time written on the reverse side
Pencil and paper

Front

Back

Directions to the Learner

1   Sort the cards so all the clocks face up.
2   Look at the top card and write the time it
    shows in numbers on your paper.
3   Turn the card over to check your answer.
4   After completing all the cards, mix them up.
5   Sort the cards so all the times written in num-
    bers face up.
6   Now try to draw the clocks and check your
    answers.

Cassette: Subtraction Facts

Pinpoint

Hear "number minus number" of basic subtraction facts 0–18—
write the difference

Aim

To compute subtraction facts at the rate of 40 digits per minute
with two or fewer errors

Feedback Device

After the problems have been delivered for one minute, the answers are given orally on the tape. The learner checks what he
hears against what he wrote.

Materials

Cassette tape recorder
Cassette tape prepared with subtraction problems given
in 1-minute segments which gradually increase in
speed; the problems are stated in this form: "seven minus six, eleven minus five . . . ;" answers follow each
segment
Pencil and paper

Directions to the Learner

[Record on the tape]
1 Get your pencil and paper ready.
2 You will hear subtraction problems given at a
steady pace for 1 minute.
3 Write down as many answers as you can.
4 Listen for the answers.
5 If you have more than two incorrect answers,
rewind the tape and review the same
problems.

6 If you have two or less incorrect answers, go on to the next set of problems on the tape. They are given at a little faster rate. Try your best!

Colored Acetate Folder: Addition

Pinpoint

See math problem of 3 digits plus 3 digits with regrouping—
write sum

Aim

To compute addition problems at the rate of 40 digits per minute
with two or fewer errors

Feedback Device

When the worksheet is in the colored folder, only the problems
can be seen. After writing the sums on the acetate folder with a
grease pencil, the student removes the worksheet from its folder
to check the answers.

Materials

Colored (red) acetate folder with a binder
Grease pencil or washable acetate marker
Worksheet prepared with the two addends written in
dark ink and the answers written with a yellow felt-tip
marker

348	981	467	117	639	894
+573	+322	+129	+211	+412	+367
559	602	272	591	534	740
+133	+128	+541	+694	+109	+378
619	490	585	362	752	294
+883	+214	+717	+475	+197	+136

binder

yellow answers
cannot be seen

Red folder
with worksheet inside

Directions to the Learner

1 Put the worksheet inside the folder.
2 Write your answers on the folder with the special pen or pencil.
3 When you have finished, pull the worksheet out of the folder and check your answers with the answers written in yellow.
4 Take some practice timings.

Flap: Measurement

Pinpoint

See two linear measurements—write < or > to describe their relationship

Aim

To select the correct symbol describing the relationship between two linear measurements

Feedback Device

A flap covers the answer when the stimulus cards are behind the cover card. After writing a response, the student lifts the flap to reveal the answer.

Materials

Stiff piece of cardboard, approximately 3″ x 5″, with two open holes cut near the top and one hole cut near the bottom covered with a flap of vinyl or fabric

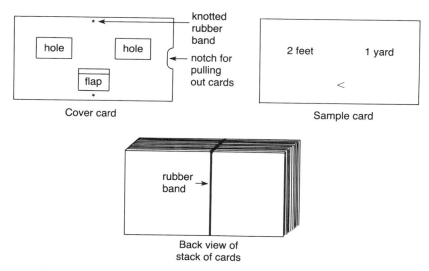

Cover card

Sample card

Back view of stack of cards

3" x 5" stimulus cards containing two linear measure-ments near the top and the appropriate symbol near the bottom; the cards are held behind the cover card with a large rubber band

Pencil and paper

Directions to the Learner

1   Make sure all the cards are facing the same way.
2   Put the index cards behind the cover card and inside the rubber band. Be sure you can see the two parts of the problem in the windows.
3   Look at the two measurements showing in the windows and decide which is longer.
4   On your paper, write the symbol that tells how the two measurements relate, $<$ or $>$.
5   After you have written your answer, raise the flap to check your response with the answer on the card.
6   Pull the top card out and go on to the next problem.

Holes: Basic Addition Facts

Pinpoint

See one digit plus one digit—write sum

Aim

To complete addition facts 0–18 with 100 percent accuracy

Feedback Device

When the student puts his pencil in the hole of the problem he has worked and turns over the board, the correct answer is written next to the hole where his pencil is.

Materials

Figure cut out of tagboard with holes punched at random, a number placed near each hole, an operation sign and a number written in the middle of the figure, and answers on the back beside the holes
Pencil and paper

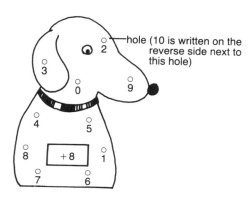

hole (10 is written on the reverse side next to this hole)

45

Directions to the Learner

1. On your own paper, add 8 to all the numbers 0–9.
2. Check your answers by putting your pencil in the hole beside a number and turning the figure over to find the answer beside the hole.

Suggestions to the Teacher

Each side of the figure can be used as the problem or the answer. In the example, on one side, students may practice adding 8 to each number; on the other side, they may practice subtracting 8 from each number.

Light: Lowest Common Denominator

Pinpoint

See two fractions with different denominators—write the lowest common denominator

Aim

To find the lowest common denominator of two fractions with 80 percent accuracy

Feedback Device

The student selects a response and inserts the stylus in the hole above it. If the choice is correct, the light comes on.

Materials

Electric Learning Board (see chapter 2 for a list of materials and construction guidelines)

5″ x 8″ stimulus cards showing two fractions and three lowest common denominator choices

Pencil and paper

Directions to the Learner

[Write on cover card for the pack]

1 Place one card on the board by lining up the arrow on the card with the arrow on the board.

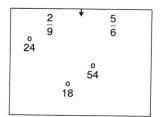 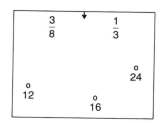

Sample cards

2 Find the lowest common denominator for the two fractions at the top of the card.

3 Work each problem on your own paper and write your answer.

4 Choose one of the three numbers on the card as your answer by putting the stylus in the hole above the number. If your answer is correct and the wiring is intact, the light will come on. Yea!

5 If there is no light, try other answers. Then put the card on the bottom of the pile to review later.

Matching: Missing Addends

Pinpoint

See problem with missing addend—clip number that completes
the problem to the board

Aim

To complete all the missing addend problems with 100%
accuracy

Feedback Device

When the clothespin containing the correct answer is clipped to
the problem on the board and the board is turned over, the symbol on the back of the clothespin matches the symbol on the back
of the board.

Materials

Segmented cardboard showing problems on the front
   and symbols on the back
Clothespins with answers on one side and symbols corresponding to the correct section of the board on the
   other side

Directions to the Learner

1 Match the number on the clothespin to the
problem it answers.

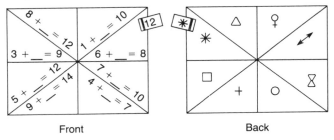

Front   Back

2 Clip the clothespin to the section of the board containing the problem it answers.

3 Turn the board over. If the answer is correct, the symbols on the clothespin and the board match.

Pockets: Word Problems

Pinpoint

See word problem—select correct operation and write answer to calculation

Aim

To complete the word problems with 90% accuracy

Feedback Device

After reading the problem, the student says which operation is necessary to complete the problem. To check this step, he inserts the card into the pocket. Holes at different levels indicate the four operations, and a line shows in the hole next to the correct operation for the problem. The answer to the calculation is on the back of the card.

Materials

Pocket made from tagboard with four holes punched in the front of the pocket and an operation sign (+, −, ×, ÷) written next to each hole

Stimulus cards with a word problem written on the top of the card, an appropriately placed line across the bottom of the card to indicate the correct operation, and the correct answer written on the back of the card

Pencil and paper

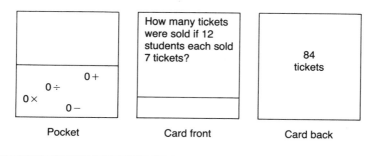

Pocket	Card front	Card back

Directions to the Learner

1 Take all the cards out of the pocket.
2 Read the first problem and decide which operation is needed to complete the problem (addition, subtraction, multiplication, or division).
3 Insert the card in the pocket and a line will show in a hole to indicate which operation is correct.
4 Do the calculation on your own paper.
5 Check your answer with the answer on the back of the card.

Puzzles: Geometric Figures

Pinpoint

See geometric figure—write name
See name of geometric figure—draw example of figure

Aim

To correctly name and/or draw all of the figures

Feedback Device

After looking at only the figures (or only the names) and writing a response, the student completes the two-piece puzzles by matching each figure with its name and then checks the correct answers.

Materials

Laminated index cards each cut into two irregular pieces with one piece showing a geometric figure and the corresponding piece giving the figure's name
Pencil and paper

Directions to the Learner

1 Sort the pieces into two piles according to shapes and names.
2 Take the shape pieces and for each one write the name of the figure.
3 Place the shape pieces on your desk in the order you looked at them.

Sample cards

4 After writing answers for each piece, complete each two-piece puzzle with the name pieces.

5 Check your answers with each finished puzzle.

6 When you get all the names right, try looking at the name pieces and drawing the shapes.

Strips in a Folder: Multiplication

Pinpoint

See problem of two digits multiplied by one digit—write product

Aim

To compute multiplication problems at the rate of 40 digits per minute with two or fewer errors

Feedback Device

After writing answers on the laminated strips, the learner pulls the worksheet upward to reveal the answers.

Materials

Laminated manila folder with strips cut out across the front
Grease pencil
Worksheet of multiplication problems and answers

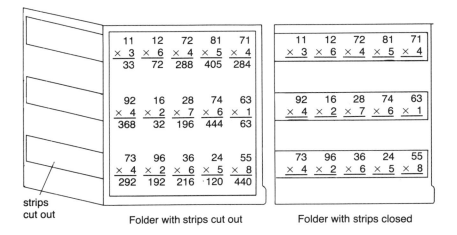

strips
cut out

Folder with strips cut out   Folder with strips closed

Directions to the Learner

1 Insert the worksheet in the folder so that only the problems show.
2 Work each problem and write your answer with a grease pencil on the laminated folder. Write any numbers you carry on the folder above the problem.
3 Pull the worksheet up and check your answers.
4 For practice, take some 1-minute timings.

Stylus: Place Value

Pinpoint

See question about place value of numbers—select correct answer hole with a stylus

Aim

To achieve 50% of the adult rate on the place value task, with 90% accuracy

Feedback Device

The student inserts a pencil in one of the holes below the answer and pulls the card to see if it comes out of the box. If the right hole is selected, the card is easily removed from the box.

Materials

Cardboard or wooden box big enough to hold index cards (see Poke Box presented in chapter 2, but make four evenly spaced holes across the front of the box)
Large rubber band
Stylus, pencil, or thin stick
Stimulus cards with place value questions at the top of the card and answer choices above punched out holes at the bottom of the card (include at least enough stimulus cards to last through a 1-minute timing)

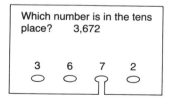
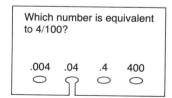

Sample cards

Directions to the Learner

[Write on the top card of the deck]

1 Read the question on the card.
2 Choose your answer by poking the stylus in the hole under it.
3 Pull gently on the card. It will come out the box if your answer is right. If your answer is not right, choose again until you find the correct answer. Put missed cards back in the box for another try.
4 Repeat the task with all the cards.
5 For practice, take 1-minute timings.

Windows: Money

Pinpoint

See pictures of coins and amounts in numbers—match equivalents

Aim

To complete the puzzle successfully by matching coins and amounts

Feedback Device

When the puzzle is completed correctly and viewed through the window, a message appears.

Materials

6″ x 8″ piece of poster board cut into puzzle pieces showing coins and amounts in numbers

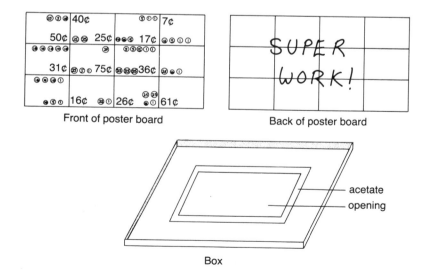

Front of poster board   Back of poster board

Box

Piece of cardboard or a box with a 7″ x 10″ opening cut in
  it
8½″ x 11″ piece of acetate covering the 7″ x 10″ opening
  in the box
Envelope to hold the puzzle pieces

Directions to the Learner

[Write on the envelope]

1 Sort all the pieces so the numbers face up.
2 Match the coins to the same amount in numbers.
3 Make the puzzle on top of the window in the box.
4 When you have finished, lift the box and look in the window. If the secret message appears, you completed the puzzle correctly.

Arithmetic Scope and Sequence Skills List*

Key:
1D = one-digit number   < = less than
2D = two-digit number   > = more than
3D = three-digit number   ≤ = less than or equal to

Addition Hierarchy

Recognizes inequalities of numbers less than 10
Understands seriation of numbers less than 10
Recognizes the words *addend* and *sum*
Understands the " + " sign
Computes sums less than 10 (should be memorized)
Understands place value of ones and tens
Computes sums for numbers 10–18, both addends less than 10 (should be memorized)
Computes 2D + 1D without regrouping
Computes 2D + 2D without regrouping
Understands place value concerning regrouping tens and ones
Computes 2D + 1D with regrouping
Computes 2D + 2D with regrouping
Computes 2D + 2D + 2D with sums of ones greater than 20
Understands place value of hundreds, tens, and ones
Computes 3D + 3D without regrouping
Understands place value concerning regrouping hundreds and tens
Computes 3D + 3D with regrouping
Estimates sums

---

*Source. From *Teaching Students with Learning Problems* by C. D. Mercer and A. R. Mercer. Columbus, Ohio: Charles E. Merrill, 1981, pp. 395–401. Reprinted by permission. Portions of this skills list were adapted from *Diagnosing Mathematical Difficulties* by R. Underhill, E. Uprichard, and J. Heddens. Columbus, Ohio: Charles E. Merrill, 1980, pp. 262–67, 278–90. Reprinted by permission.

Subtraction Hierarchy

Finds missing addends (for example, $4 + \underline{\quad} = 9$)

Understands the " $-$ " sign

Uses set separation as model for subtraction

Expresses a related addition statement in subtraction form (addend + *addend* = sum $\leftrightarrow$ sum $-$ *addend* = addend)

Relates the words *minuend, subtrahend,* and *difference* to *sum, given addend,* and *missing addend*

Memorizes basic subtraction facts for numbers 0–9

Understands place value of ones and tens

Memorizes basic subtraction facts for numbers 0–18

Names the difference between a two-place whole number (2D) and a one-place whole number (1D) (not a basic fact and no regrouping)

Names the difference between 2D and 2D with no regrouping

Names the difference between 3D and 2D with no regrouping

Names the difference between 3D and 3D with no regrouping

Names the difference between two many-digit whole numbers with no regrouping

Names the difference between 2D and 1D (not a basic fact) with regrouping

Names the difference between 2D and 2D with regrouping from tens to ones

Names the difference between 3D and 2D with regrouping from tens to ones

Names the difference between 3D and 2D with double regrouping

Names the difference between 3D and 3D with single regrouping

Names the difference between 3D and 3D with double regrouping

Names the difference between two many-place whole numbers with several regroupings

Names the difference when a zero appears in a single place in the minuend

Names the difference when zeros appear in the tens and ones place of the minuend

Estimates differences

Multiplication Hierarchy

Recognizes sets as models for multiplication (number of sets and number of objects in each set)

Recognizes and uses arrays as a model for multiplication; for example,

```
  2
× ×
× ×   3
× ×
```

Understands the words *factor* and *product*

Understands the " × " sign

Understands the commutative property of multiplication; for example, $a \times (b + c) = (a \times b) + (a \times c)$ [$a \le 5$, $b \le 5$]

Memorizes basic multiplication facts for $a \times b$ ($a \le 5$, $b \le 5$)

Memorizes basic multiplication facts for $a \times b$ ($5 < a < 10$, $b < 10$)

Names the product if one factor is 10, 100, etc.

Expands the basic multiplication facts (for example, 4×3 to 4×30)

Computes 2D × 1D without regrouping

Understands place value of tens, ones, regrouping

Computes $a \times (b + c) = (a \times b) + (a \times c)$ [$a < 10$, $a \times (b + c) < 100$ with regrouping] (for example, $6 \times (10 + 3) = \underline{\quad} + \underline{\quad} = \underline{\quad}$)

Computes 2D × 1D with regrouping, product < 100

Understands place value of hundreds, tens, ones

Computes 2D × 1D with regrouping, product < 100

Computes 2D × 2D with regrouping

Computes 3D × 1D with regrouping

Computes 3D × 2D with regrouping

Division Hierarchy

Finds missing factor (for example, $6 \times \underline{\quad} = 36$)

Uses symbols which indicate division ($2\overline{)6}$, $6 \div 2$, $\%$)

Expresses a related multiplication sentence as a division sentence (product + factor = factor)

Computes division facts with one as divisor (for example, $1\overline{)6}$)

Computes basic division facts (a ÷ b where a ≤ 81, b ≤ 9)

Computes division of a nonzero number by itself (for example, 12)12̄)

Computes 1D ÷ 1D with a remainder

Estimates 2D ÷ 1D and computes 2D ÷ 1D with a remainder

Computes quotients with expanding dividend (for example, 3)9̄, 3)90̄, 3)900̄)

Estimates 3D ÷ 1D and computes 3D ÷ 1D (for example, 6)747̄)

Computes quotient of many-place dividend with a one-place divisor (for example, 4)78743̄)

Estimates 3D ÷ 2D and computes 3D ÷ 2D where divisor is multiple of 10 (for example, 20)684̄)

Computes quotient with divisors of 100, 1000, etc. (for example, 1000)6897̄)

Estimates 3D ÷ 2D and computes 3D ÷ 2D (for example, 17)489̄)

Computes quotient of many-place dividend and many-place divisor (for example, 3897)487876̄)

Fraction Hierarchy

Readiness Areas

Separates regions into subregions that are equivalent

Expresses "1" in many different ways

Uses the terms *fraction, fraction bar, numerator,* and *denominator*

Models, on the number line, equivalent fractions

Generates sets of equivalent fractions

Renames fractions in simplest form

Rewrites improper fractions as mixed numerals

Rewrites mixed numerals as improper fractions

Develops concept of least common denominator using the concept of least common multiple

Compares fractional numbers

Develops concept of least common denominator using the concept of greatest common factor

Addition

Computes sums of less than 1, with fractions having the same denominator

Computes sums of mixed numerals, with no regrouping and same denominator

Computes sums between 1 and 2, with same denominator and regrouping

Computes sums of mixed numeral and nonunit fraction, with regrouping and same denominator (for example, $3\frac{2}{5} + \frac{4}{5}$)

Computes sums of mixed numerals with regrouping and same denominator (for example, $8\frac{3}{5} + 2\frac{4}{5}$)

Computes sums of less than 1 with different denominators

Computes sums of mixed numerals, with no regrouping and different denominators

Computes sums of mixed numerals, with regrouping and different denominators

Computes sums of three nonunit fractions with different denominators

Solves word problems requiring addition of fractions

Subtraction

Computes differences between two fractions with like denominators without regrouping, then with regrouping

Computes differences between two fractions with unlike but related denominators without regrouping, then with regrouping

Computes differences between two fractions with unlike and unrelated denominators without regrouping, then with regrouping

Solves word problems requiring subtraction of fractions

Multiplication

Computes product of whole number $\times$ unit fraction, with product < 1 (for example, $3 \times \frac{1}{4} = $ ___)

Computes product of whole number $\times$ nonunit fraction, with product < 1 (for example, $2 \times \frac{2}{5} = $ ___)

Gives fraction names for one (for example, $1 = \frac{?}{7}$)

Solves regrouping problem by writing fraction as mixed numeral, $1 < a < 2$ (for example, $\frac{7}{5} = $ ___)

Computes product of whole number $\times$ nonunit fraction, $1 < $ product < 2 (for example, $\frac{7}{5} = 3 \times \frac{3}{5} = $ ___)

Computes product of unit fraction $\times$ unit fraction (for example, $\frac{1}{3} \times \frac{1}{4} = $ ___)

Computes product of nonunit fraction $\times$ nonunit fraction (for example, $\frac{2}{3} \times \frac{4}{5} = $ ___)

Computes $a \times (b + c) = (a \times b) + (a \times c)$, when a and b are whole numbers and c is a unit fraction, with no regrouping (for example, $3 \times (2 + \frac{1}{4}) = $ ___ $ + $ ___)

Computes $a \times (b + c) = (a \times b) + (a \times c)$, when a and b are whole numbers and c is a nonunit fraction, with regrouping (for example, $4 \times 3\frac{2}{5} = 4 \times (3 + \frac{2}{5}) = $ ___ + ___ = ___)

Computes product of nonunit fraction $\times$ mixed numeral using improper fractions—for example, $\frac{5}{6} \times 2\frac{1}{3}$ (change to improper fractions)

Computes product of mixed numeral $\times$ mixed numeral using improper fractions—for example, $3\frac{3}{4} \times 1\frac{7}{8}$ (use improper fractions)

Division

Computes quotient of $1 \div$ unit fraction (for example, $1 \div \frac{1}{5}$)

Computes quotient of whole number $\div$ nonunit fraction, when $1 <$ whole number < 10—for example, $2 \div \frac{3}{5}$ (use repeated subtraction and remainder as fractional part)

Computes $\frac{1}{a} \div \frac{1}{b}$ where a $<$ b (common denominator approach) (for example, $\frac{1}{2} \div \frac{1}{3}$)

Computes $\frac{a}{b} \div \frac{c}{d}$ (common denominator approach) (for example, $\frac{3}{5} \div \frac{3}{4}$)

Computes quotient of two mixed numerals (common denominator approach) (for example, $2\frac{1}{5} \div 1\frac{2}{3}$)

Decimal Hierarchy

Readiness Areas

Generates decimal place value by rewriting fractions with denominators of powers of 10

Recognizes decimal place value to millionths place

Reads and writes rational numbers expressed as decimals

Rewrites fractions as decimals

Models rational numbers expressed as decimals using the number line

Generates equivalent decimals by appending zeros

Addition

Names the sum of two rational numbers expressed as decimals having the same place value

Names the sum of two rational numbers expressed as decimals having different place values

Names the sum of more than two rational numbers expressed as decimals having different place values

Solves word problems requiring addition of rational numbers expressed as decimals

Subtraction

Names the difference between two rational numbers expressed as decimals having the same place value (without regrouping and with regrouping)

Names the difference between two rational numbers expressed as decimals having different place values (without regrouping and with regrouping)

Solves word problems requiring subtraction of rational numbers expressed as decimals

Multiplication

Names the product of two rational numbers expressed as decimals when it is necessary to append zeroes to the left of a nonzero digit as decimal holders

Names the product of more than two rational numbers expressed as decimals

Solves word problems requiring multiplication of rational numbers expressed as decimals

Division

Names the quotient of rational numbers expressed as decimals when the divisor is a whole number

Names the quotient of any two rational numbers expressed as decimals by using the division algorithm

Solves word problems requiring division of rational numbers expressed as decimals

Percents

Interprets the symbol for percent (%) as a fraction and as a decimal

Rewrites percents as decimals and fractions for percents less than 100% and then for percents equal to or greater than 100%

Rewrites fractions or decimals as percents

Solves word problems requiring percents

Money Hierarchy

Identifies coins

Recognizes relative value of coins

Makes change for amounts up to $1.00

Recognizes and uses money notation
Recognizes currency and makes change for currency
Solves examples and word problems involving money

Time Hierarchy

Relates the face of the clock to the number line through 12 for hours
Relates the face of the clock to the number line through 60 for minutes
Tells time by the hour
Tells time by the minute
Understands the difference between A.M. and P.M.
Solves examples and word problems involving time

Measurement Hierarchy

Linear

Uses a straightedge of arbitrary length to measure an object
Makes a ruler of at least 12″ with 1″ markings
Uses an inch-marked ruler to measure items
Recognizes that 12 inches measures the same length as 1 foot
Identifies measurements of objects which are less than, greater than, or equal to 1 foot
Introduces the symbols for inches and feet
Makes a ruler with ½″ and ¼″ markings to measure objects
Uses a ruler with ½″ and ¼″ markings to measure objects
Estimates heights and lengths in feet and/or inches
Recognizes and compares the lengths of inch, foot, yard, and mile
Solves examples involving denominate numbers related to linear measurement
Solves word problems applying the concepts of linear measurement
Recognizes metric units and relates them to one another

Liquid and Dry

Recognizes relationships between and relative values of cup, pint, quart, half-gallon, and gallon

Recognizes metric units and relates them to one another

Solves examples involving denominate numbers related to liquid or dry measurements

Solves word problems involving liquid measurement

Weight

Compares relative weights of objects using a balance

Recognizes relationships between and relative values of ounce, pound, and ton

Weighs objects to nearest pound and ounce

Uses the abbreviations *oz., lb.,* and *T.* in recording weights

Recognizes metric units and relates them to one another

Solves examples involving denominate numbers related to weight measurement

Solves word problems involving weight measurements

LANGUAGE MATERIALS

This chapter illustrates the use of self-correcting materials with selected language skills. Language development is complex and includes a multitude of specific skills. For this reason, a language scope and sequence skills network, presented at the end of this chapter, will help the instructor understand the general development of language and plan individualized interventions. This network includes phonology, morphology, syntax, semantics, and pragmatics. Moreover, detailed scope and sequence skills lists in commercial language programs and/or tests are helpful in identifying specific skills to use with self-correcting materials.

Answer on Back: Employment Vocabulary

Pinpoint

See definition of term common to job applications and interviews—say term

Aim

To say employment terms correctly in a demonstration for the teacher after practicing with the self-correcting material

Feedback Device

A term is written on one side of a card, and its definition is written on the reverse side.

Materials

Index cards prepared with a definition of an employment term written on one side and the corresponding term (for example, *experience, minimum wage, application, reference, benefits*) written on the reverse side.

Directions to the Learner

[Write on top card of the deck]
1 Sort all the cards so the definitions face up.
2 Read a definition and say the term it describes.
3 Look on the back of the card to see if you are correct. Your goal is to do all the cards correctly in a demonstration for the teacher.

the name and address of someone who can recommend you for a job	reference
Front	Back

Cassette: Following Oral Directions

Pinpoint

Hear taped instructions—draw figure

Aim

To reproduce each figure exactly, according to the directions given on the cassette tape

Feedback Device

Correct figures are drawn on clear acetate with a permanent marker. After listening to directions and drawing a figure, the learner places the corresponding acetate over his work to check the lines he drew.

Materials

Cassette tape recorder
Cassette tape prepared with directions (given slowly) for
    drawing various figures
Graph paper and pencil
Folder containing acetate pages with drawings corre-
    sponding to the figures presented on the tape

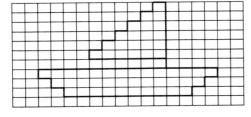

"Count from the top left edge over 6 lines and draw an X. (Pause.) Start drawing here. Go down 7 spaces (pause), right 4 (pause), down 1 (pause), left 1 (pause), down 1 . . ."

Figure   Instructions

Directions to the Learner

[Give at the beginning of the tape]

1 Get your piece of graph paper and pencil ready.

2 Listen to and follow the instructions. A picture will appear.

3 To check if you have followed the instructions correctly, get the acetate for the corresponding drawing from the folder, and line up the arrow with where you started. The drawings should match.

Colored Acetate Folder: Indirect Request

Pinpoint

See sentences—draw a circle by the questions or draw an X by indirect requests

Aim

To mark questions and indirect requests with one or no errors in a 1-minute timing

Feedback Device

According to the directions, sentences on a probe are marked with a yellow marker. When the probe is inside a colored acetate folder, the answers are invisible. After the student completes the page or timing with a grease pencil on the acetate, the sheet is removed from the folder. The student makes a side-by-side comparison of the given answers and his work.

X = indirect request;		
O = question for information		answers written
1. What time is it?	O	in yellow
2. Can you shut the door?	X	
3. Won't you stop that?	X	
4. Can't you finish your work?	X	
5. When does the bus arrive?	O	
6. Is the water running?	O	
7. Must you just sit there?	X	
8. Must you slurp your milk?	X	
9. Can't you sit still?	X	
10. Did the dog run away?	O	

Sample probe

75

Materials

Colored acetate folder (red is best)
Grease pencil or washable acetate marker
Probe with correct responses marked with a yellow felt-
tip marker

Directions to the Learner

[Write on the reverse side of the probe]

1 Place this page inside a colored acetate folder.
2 Take a few seconds to look at the probe.
3 Do all writing with a grease pencil or acetate
marker.
4 Write an X beside a sentence if it is an indirect
request for someone to do something.
5 Write an O beside a sentence that asks for
information.
6 Take a practice timing.
7 Take a 1-minute timing and record your rate.
8 Remove the page from the folder and compare
your answers with those written in yellow.

Flap: Suffixes (-less and -ful)

Pinpoint

See incomplete sentence—write correct suffix (-less or -ful)

Aim

To use the suffixes *-less* and *-ful* correctly in 10 sentences

Feedback Device

The correct answer is revealed under a flap.

Materials

Laminated card that contains incomplete sentences which require a root word and the suffix *-less* or *-ful*

Laminated card illustrating a tree with roots at the bottom and the same number of branches at the top of the tree: (a) two numbered leaves on each branch are cut so that each leaf will fold back to reveal an answer underneath; (b) holes are punched in each corner of the card and a sheet of paper is attached to the back of the card with brass fasteners; (c) under each numbered leaf a suffix is written that matches up with the respective sentence; and (d) root words are written along the tree roots with a grease pencil

Grease pencil

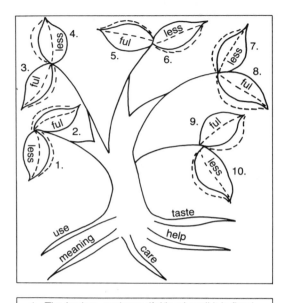

Sample cards

1. The broken car is use(ful/less) until it is fixed.
2. The basket is use(ful/less) to carry groceries.
3. I learned a lot from the meaning(ful/less) speech.
4. The poor directions were meaning(ful/less).
5. The student was very care(ful/less) and wrote a neat letter.
6. The student was care(ful/less) and spilled paint on her dress.
7. She felt help(ful/less) when she couldn't start her car.
8. The neighbor was help(ful/less) when she loaned me her telephone.
9. The flower arrangement was pleasing and taste(ful/less).
10. The food was very bland and taste(ful/less) to me.

Directions to the Learner

1 Read each sentence on the card and circle the correct suffix with the grease pencil.

2 Check your answers by lifting each leaf on the tree to see the correct answer underneath. The answers are numbered to match the sentences.

Holes: Past-Tense Morpheme (-ed)

Pinpoint

See sentence with verb in past tense (*-ed* form)—write $\underline{Y}$ (yes) or $\underline{N}$ (no) to indicate whether or not the verb is used correctly

Aim

To indicate with 90% accuracy if the verb in past tense is used correctly

Feedback Device

The correct response ($\underline{Y}$ or $\underline{N}$) is written on the back of the worksheet beside each hole. After the student writes his responses, he lines up his paper with the back of the worksheet and checks the answers.

Materials

Worksheet attached to half of a manila folder with a hole punched next to each sentence and the answers written on the back of the folder beside each hole

Pencil and paper

Directions to the Learner

1 Place the worksheet over a piece of paper.
2 Read each sentence and decide if the under-lined word is used correctly.

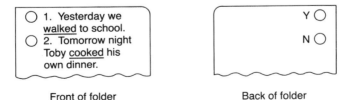

Front of folder   Back of folder

3 If your answer is yes, write $\underline{Y}$ in the hole beside the sentence. If it is no, write $\underline{N}$.

4 After you have written an answer for each sentence, turn the worksheet over. Line up your answers next to the holes and check to see if your letters ($\underline{Y}$ or $\underline{N}$) match the answers on the back of the folder.

Light: Analogies

Pinpoint

See incomplete analogy—select correct word from four choices to complete analogy

Aim

To answer successfully 90% of the analogy problems in a demonstration for the teacher

Feedback Device

A card is placed on top of a specially wired board. The student selects an answer by inserting the stylus in a hole. If the choice is correct, a circuit is completed and a bulb lights up as a signal to the learner.

Materials

Electric Learning Board (see chapter 2 for a list of materials and construction guidelines)

5″ x 8″ stimulus cards containing incomplete analogies and four answer choices

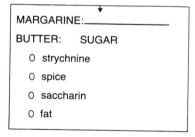

MARGARINE:_____

BUTTER: SUGAR

  O strychnine

  O spice

  O saccharin

  O fat

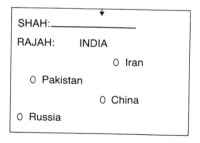

SHAH:_____

RAJAH: INDIA

               O Iran

  O Pakistan

               O China

 O Russia

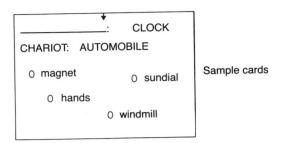

_____: CLOCK

CHARIOT: AUTOMOBILE

O magnet

O sundial

O hands

O windmill

Sample cards

Directions to the Learner

[Write on the top card of the deck]

1 Place each card on the Electric Learning Board and line up the arrow on the card with the arrow on the board.

2 Read the analogy problem and indicate an answer by placing the stylus in the hole next to your choice. If your choice is correct, a circuit is completed, and the light will come on.

Matching: Cause and Effect

Pinpoint

See sentences describing events—match a cause to its effect

Aim

To match successfully all cause/effect pairs by placing the cause before the effect in a demonstration for the classroom teacher or aide

Feedback Device

When flipped over, the cards will form a complete picture if the cause/effect pair is laid down in the correct order.

Materials

8″ x 5″ index cards which are cut in half after a cause sentence is written on one half, an effect sentence is written on the other half, and a magazine picture is pasted on the reverse side

Two large pieces of stiff cardboard slightly larger than 8″ x 5″

Directions to the Learner

1 Sort all the cards so the printing is face up.
2 Find two cards that match a cause and an effect.

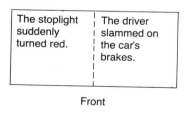

Front

Back

3 On one piece of cardboard, place the cause card to the left and then place the effect card to its right.

4 Place the second piece of cardboard on the top of the cards.

5 Turn the cardboards over and take off the top one. You matched the correct cards if a whole picture appears.

Pockets: Verb Tense

Pinpoint

See sentence and illustration—classify verb form as past, present, or future tense

Aim

To classify all verbs on the cards correctly

Feedback Device

After sorting the cards into three envelopes, the student checks to see if the symbols on the backs of the cards match the ones on the envelopes.

Materials

Three envelopes (large enough to hold 3″ x 5″ index cards) for present-, past-, and future-tense verbs with a different symbol on each envelope

Set of 3″ x 5″ index cards with a sentence and a picture of the time-related verb tense on the front of the card and the symbol corresponding to the correct tense on the back of the card

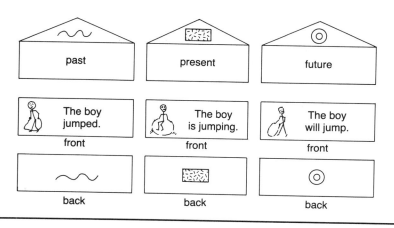

Directions to the Learner

1 Shuffle the cards and then sort them so the printing is face up.
2 Lay out the three envelopes in this order: past, present, future.
3 Take one card and read the sentence and look at the picture.
4 Decide when the action happened. Put the card in the envelope that tells when the action happened.
5 When all the cards are in envelopes, look at the symbols on the backs of the cards. If they match the symbols on the top of the envelopes, your answers are right.

Puzzles: Interrogative Reversal

Pinpoint

See a sentence—write its interrogative reversal

Aim

To write 90% of the questions correctly after practicing with the self-correcting material

Feedback Device

The pieces of the puzzle fit together when the sentence is in question form.

Materials

Worksheet with declarative sentences
Strips of tagboard (2″ wide) clipped together, containing puzzle pieces of the interrogative reversal of the corresponding declarative sentence
Pencil

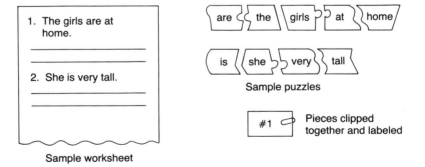

1. The girls are at home.

2. She is very tall.

Sample worksheet

are the girls at home

is she very tall

Sample puzzles

#1   Pieces clipped together and labeled

Directions to the Learner

1. Rewrite each sentence on the worksheet as a question on the lines below the sentence.

2. Check your answer by putting the puzzle pieces together. They are clipped together and numbered to match the sentences on the worksheet. The puzzles form the correct questions.

3. Clip the pieces together with the correct labels for the next person. Thanks!

Strips in a Folder: Sentence Order

Pinpoint

See a group of words—write the words in an order that forms a meaningful sentence

Aim

To write meaningful sentences from groups of words presented on a worksheet

Feedback Device

The answers are covered by the folder's strips and are revealed when the worksheet is pulled upward.

Materials

Laminated manila folder with strips cut out across the front
Worksheet with groups of words written in black lettering and a meaningful sentence written in yellow lettering underneath each respective group
Grease pencil

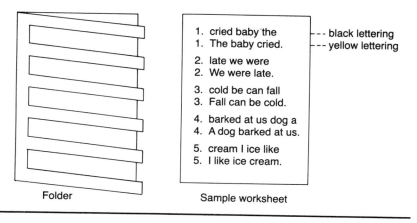

1. cried baby the
1. The baby cried.

2. late we were
2. We were late.

3. cold be can fall
3. Fall can be cold.

4. barked at us dog a
4. A dog barked at us.

5. cream I ice like
5. I like ice cream.

--- black lettering
--- yellow lettering

Folder   Sample worksheet

Directions to the Learner

1 Look at the first group of words.
2 Use all the words to form a complete sentence.
3 Using the grease pencil, write your sentence on the strip underneath the group of words.
4 When all the sentences are completed, pull the worksheet up just far enough to see the answers written in yellow.

Stylus: Deep Structure

Pinpoint

See pairs of sentences—insert a stylus into a hole to indicate if the sentences have the same or different meanings

Aim

To determine with 90% accuracy if sentences have same or different meanings after daily practice sessions with the self-correcting material

Feedback Device

Cards containing holes below incorrect responses and slots below correct ones are placed in a box with corresponding holes. The student makes a response by pushing the stylus in one of the holes. If the card is easily pulled from the box, the response is correct.

Materials

Large cardboard or wooden box (see Poke Box in chapter 2, but make two evenly spaced holes across the front of the box)
Large rubber band
Stylus, pencil, or thin stick
Stimulus cards with pairs of sentences written at the top of the card and *same* and *different* written above punched out holes at the bottom of the card

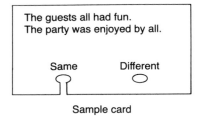

Sample card

Directions to the Learner

[Write on the top card in the deck]

1 Read the pair of sentences on a card.
2 Decide if the meaning of the two sentences is the same or different.
3 Insert the stylus in the hole below your answer.
4 Pull gently on the card. If it comes out of the deck easily, your answer is correct.
5 Try all the cards. Your goal is to answer correctly 45 out of 50 cards.

Windows: Opposites

Pinpoint

See picture—find picture of its opposite

Aim

To demonstrate for the teacher the correct opposite match for all the pictures on a single wheel

Feedback Device

When a correct match is displayed in the front windows, the symbols in the back windows match.

Materials

Spinning Wheels (see chapter 2 for list of materials and construction guidelines) with wheel sets of picture opposites

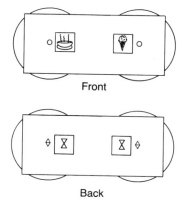

Front

Back

Directions to the Learner

1 Look at the side of the Spinning Wheels that has pictures.

2 Turn the wheels until you see two pictures that are opposites.

3 Check your answer by looking on the back to see if the symbols in the windows match.

Language Scope and Sequence Skills List*

Developmental Age: 1–3 Years

Phonology

> Uses first consonants—/p/, /m/, /t/, and /k/
> Uses first vowels—/a/, /i/, and /u/

Morphology

> Uses first words pertaining to parents, objects, etc.; declarative, imperative, and interrogative functions

Syntax

> Uses sentence-like word, for example, word is combined with nonverbal cues (gestures and inflections—"Mommy," "Mommy!," "Mommy?") (12–18 months)
> Uses first two-word grammatical utterance (18–24 months)
> Uses three- or four-word utterances (24–36 months)
> Includes both subject and predicate in the sentence types: "She's a pretty baby" (declarative), "Where Daddy is?" (question), "I can no play" (negative), "I want more milk" (imperative) (24–36 months)

Semantics

> Uses and understands 3–22 words (12–18 months)
> Learns general nominals, specific nominals, and action words
> Uses overextensions regarding shape, size, function, etc.
> Uses functions of words: action/state of agent, object, action/state of object, dative, object associated with object or location, location, modification of event (12–18 months)
> Uses and understands 22–272 words (18–24 months)
> Uses functions of words: agent + object, agent + action, action + object, location, nomination, possessive, attribute, nonexistence, rejection, denial, question, recurrence, acknowledgement (18–24 months)
> Uses and understands 272–896 words (24–36 months)

Source. Adapted from *Teaching Students with Learning Problems* by C. D. Mercer and A. R. Mercer. Columbus, Ohio: Charles E. Merrill, 1981, pp. 402–6. Reprinted by permission.

Understands prepositions: *in, out of, off, on, under, away from* (24–36 months)
Understands adjectives: *big, tall, soft, heavy* (24–36 months)

Pragmatics

Uses functions: instrumental, regulatory, interactional, personal, heuristic, imaginative, informative (12–18 months)

Uses intentions: labeling, responding, requesting, greeting, protesting, repeating, describing (12–18 months)

Employs verbal turn-taking procedures (12–18 months)

Uses functions: pragmatic, interpersonal, textual, ideational (18–24 months)

Responds to contingent queries (24–36 months)

Makes types of revisions as function of linguistic development (24–36 months)

Makes rapid topic change (24–36 months)

Developmental Age: 3–4 Years

Phonology

Uses /b/, /m/, /n/, /f/, /w/, /h/, /r/, /ŋ/, /p/, /t/

Morphology

Adds new words through expansion and contraction

Syntax

Adds, embeds, and permutes elements within sentences: "Read it, my book" (conjunction), "Where is Daddy?" (embedding), "I can't play" (permutation)

Uses 4 words as mean number of words per utterance

Semantics

Uses and understands 896 words

Understands prepositions: *toward, up, in front of, in back of, next to, around*

Understands adjectives: *little, big, red, black, yellow, hard, light, same, empty, more, less, high*

Pragmatics

Sustains topic

Makes systematic changes in speech depending on listener

Uses indirectives and hints

Employs productive use of contingent queries to maintain conversation

Role-plays to temporarily assume another's perspective
Has metalinguistic awareness, ability to think about language and comment on it

Developmental Age: 4–5 Years

Phonology
> Uses /p/, /d/, /g/, /k/, /y/, /l/, /t/, /b/, /r/

Syntax
> Uses 5.5 words as mean number of words per utterance.

Semantics
> Uses and understands 1540 words
> Understands prepositions: *down, beside*
> Understands adjectives: *short, fat, thin, different, low*

Developmental Age: 5–6 Years

Phonology
> Uses /v/, /s/, /z/, /ʃ/, /ʒ/

Morphology
> Uses comparative *-er*
> Uses early bound morphemes: plurals, possessives
> Uses verb tenses: present progressive, simple past, third person present, irregular past, future

Syntax
> Uses 5.7 words as mean number of words per utterance
> Subdivides word classes (nouns, verbs, and prepositions): "I would like some milk" (use of "some" with noun), "Take me to the store" (use of preposition of place)
> Begins to use complex structural distinctions

Semantics
> Uses and understands 2072 words
> Understands prepositions: *ahead of, behind*
> Understands adjectives: *first, last*

Developmental Age: 6 Years

Phonology
> Uses /t/, /θ/, /v/, /dʒ/

Morphology
> Uses regular noun plurals (balls)

Uses noun derivation -er (painter), -man (fisherman)

Uses later bound morphemes: adjective forms (comparative, superlative), deriving, diminutives, agenitives

Syntax

Uses 6.4 words as mean number of words per utterance

Embeds relative clauses with *named* or *with* (for example, I know a boy *named* John)

Semantics

Uses and understands 2562 words

Developmental Age: 7 Years

Phonology

Uses /ð/, /z/, /ʒ/, /dʒ/

Morphology

Uses adverb derivation -*ly* (easily, gently)

Syntax

Uses 7 words as mean number of words per utterance

Uses word class correctly: plural nouns, mass noun, transitive verbs

Uses complex sentence structure with relative clauses

Semantics

Uses and understands 21,600 words

Understands applying a physical term to the personality of a person (for example, a *cold* person is an unfriendly person)

Developmental Age: 8–9 Years

Phonology

Attains mature articulation

Syntax

Has occasional difficulty with the verb *promise*

Semantics

Relates word meanings directly to experiences, operations, and processes

Understands all sentences as actor-action-recipient unless the sentence is passive with a nonreversible verb; then understood as recipient-action-actor

---

Developmental Age: 10–11 Years

Syntax

Has occasional difficulty with the verb *ask* (for example, *ask* Tom what to feed the dog)

Semantics

Understands active sentences as actor-action-recipient, but interprets all passive sentences as recipient-action-actor

Developmental Age: 12 Years

Semantics

Approaches adult semantic level of word definitions

READING MATERIALS

This chapter illustrates the use of self-correcting materials in reading instruction. A reading scope and sequence skills network at the end of this chapter lists selected reading skills that self-correcting materials may help to teach. The network includes word attack and comprehension skills for grades one through six. Because self-correcting materials may be adapted to teach numerous reading skills, they enable the teacher to individualize seatwork and/or homework.

Answer on Back: Synonyms

Pinpoint

See words—cover with card containing synonym

Aim

To demonstrate for the classroom aide the ability to match correctly all the word cards with their synonyms on the board

Feedback Device

The correct answer is written in yellow on the back of each word card.

Materials

Large cardboard square, six squares across and six squares down, with a word written in each of the 36 squares

little	ended	smiled	cent	woman	trail
glad	present	cry	reply	pretty	scared
mad	large	bag	correct	distant	fast
nearly	grandma	chief	stone	speak	beach
hard	began	flat	trip	shout	odd
woods	hurry	weary	near	hungry	auto

Word cards containing synonyms for the words included on the large board and the correct responses written on the back

Plastic sandwich bag to hold word cards

Cards each containing one of the following words with the appropriate synonym from the large square written in yellow on the back:

small	finished	grinned	penny	lady	path
happy	gift	weep	answer	beautiful	afraid
angry	big	pouch	right	faraway	quick
almost	Grandmother	leader	rock	talk	shore
difficult	started	level	journey	tell	strange
forest	rush	tired	close	starved	car

Directions to the Learner

[Write on the back of the large board]

1 Sort all the word cards so the black lettering is face up.

2 Take a card and match it to its synonym on the board. Synonyms have meanings that are nearly the same.

3 After matching all the cards, turn each card over. If the word on the board matches the one written in yellow on the card, your match is correct!

Cassette: Initial Consonants

Pinpoint

Hear word—write initial consonant

Aim

To identify correctly the initial consonants of 20 words presented at the rate of one word every three seconds in a 1-minute timing

Feedback Device

The correct answers are given on the tape after a series of 20 words is presented. The learner checks the answers given on the tape with the answers he wrote.

Materials

Cassette tape recorder
Cassette tape prepared with a series of 20 words beginning with consonants, presented at the rate of one word every three seconds; answers follow the series of 20 words
Pencil and paper

Directions to the Learner

[Give on the tape]
1 Get your pencil and paper ready. Number your paper from 1 to 20.
2 Listen to each word. After you hear a word, write down the letter it starts with.
3 Listen for the answers given after the set of 20 words. Check your work.

Suggestions to the Teacher

When preparing the tape, present the words at a slower rate than the aim requires and gradually increase the rate. Provide several different word lists on the same tape. Avoid words beginning with silent letters, such as *knife* and *wrap*.

Colored Acetate Folder: Dictionary Use

Pinpoint

See word—write page number on which the word appears in the dictionary

Aim

To find vocabulary words in the dictionary

Feedback Device

When the worksheet is removed from the colored acetate folder, the answers which are written in yellow on the worksheet can be seen.

Materials

Colored (red) acetate folder
Worksheet with vocabulary words written in black and the corresponding dictionary page number written with a yellow felt-tip marker; a masking tape tab is placed at the top of the worksheet
Grease pencil or washable acetate marker
Dictionary

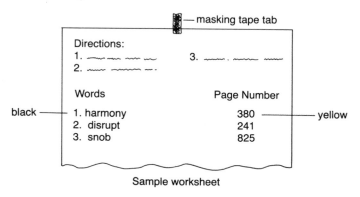

Sample worksheet

Directions to the Learner

[Write at the top of the worksheet]

1 Look up the first word in your dictionary.
2 With a grease pencil, write next to each word the page number you find the word on in the dictionary.
3 Pull the tab on the worksheet up just until the first word is above the folder. If the number in yellow matches your page number, that's great. You found the right page!

Flap: Contractions

Pinpoint

See two words—write contraction

Aim

To write correctly 90 percent of the contractions at a rate of nine words per minute when given the two words that form the contraction

Feedback Device

A flap is raised to reveal the correct response.

Materials

Laminated cardboard figure of a mouse's head with holes cut for the eyes and nose; a flexible flap of thick black felt material is held in place over the nose opening with two fasteners; three strips of cardboard are taped on the back of the mouse's head to hold the large task card of contractions in place and to allow it to slide through to present each contraction task

Task card made of cardboard with the two words to be made into a contraction written so that they will show in the eye openings and the correct answer (the contraction form) positioned in the middle column so that it will appear in the nose opening

Pencil and paper

Directions to the Learner

[Write on the back of the task card]
1   Slide this card under the strips on the back of the mouse.

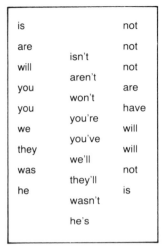

is		not
are		not
	isn't	
will		not
	aren't	
you		are
	won't	
you		have
	you're	
we		will
	you've	
they		will
	we'll	
was		not
	they'll	
he		is
	wasn't	
	he's	

Task card

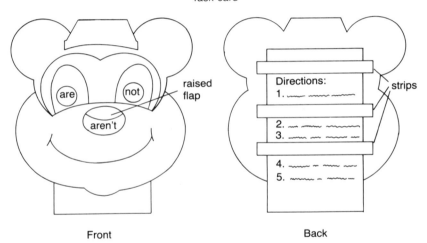

Front   Back

2 Move the card up until you can see the first two words in the eye holes.

3 Write the contraction that is formed by the two words.

4 Check your answer by raising the black felt flap to see the contraction.

5 For practice, take a 1-minute timing. Check your answers at the end of the timing.

Holes: Final Consonant Blends

Pinpoint

See incomplete word and picture—select final consonant blend from three choices

Aim

To select the correct final consonant blends for incomplete words

Feedback Device

The hole that indicates the correct answer is circled in a color on the reverse side of the card.

Materials

Index cards with a small picture or drawing at the top, the word illustrated by each picture written underneath omitting the consonant blend, and three possible answers listed next to three holes; on the back, the hole indicating the correct answer is circled in a color
Pipe cleaner

Directions to the Learner

[Write on the top card of the deck]
  1 Look at the picture on the card.

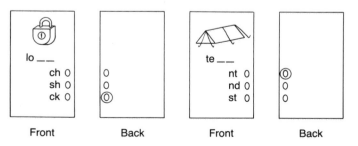

| Front | Back | Front | Back |

2   Decide which consonant blend correctly completes the label for the picture.
3   Stick the pipe cleaner through the hole next to your choice.
4   Flip the card over. If your answer is correct, the pipe cleaner will be in the colored hole.

Light: Silent Letters

Pinpoint

See word—identify any silent letters

Aim

To select with 90% accuracy the silent letters in all the words in a demonstration for the teacher

Feedback Device

When the stylus is inserted in the hole under the silent letter, the light turns on.

Materials

Electric Learning Board (see chapter 2 for a list of materials and construction guidelines)

5" x 8" stimulus cards containing words with silent letters

Directions to the Learner

[Write on the top card in the deck]
1   Place a card on the board and line up the arrow on the card with the arrow on the board.
2   Read the word and decide which letter is silent.

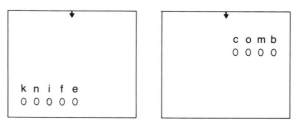

Sample cards

3 Insert the stylus in the hole under the letter you choose. If the light comes on, your answer is correct. Good work!

4 When you can select the silent letters in all the words on your first try, demonstrate this skill to the teacher.

Matching: Vocabulary

Pinpoint

See definition—match with its corresponding word

Aim

To match correctly each of 12 words with its definition

Feedback Device

The symbol on the back of the clothespin matches the symbol on
the back of the correct section of the wheel.

Materials

10-inch cardboard circle divided into 12 sections which
have definitions written in them, and a symbol on the
back of the circle in each section

12 clothespins with words corresponding to the definitions written on the front and the appropriate symbol
written on the back

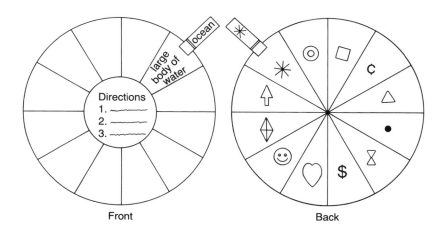

Front   Back

Directions to the Learner

[Write in the center of the circle]

1 Read a definition in one section of the wheel.

2 Match a word on a clothespin to the definition.

3 Check your answer by turning the wheel over to see if the symbols on the clothespin and the circle section match.

Pockets: Comprehending Product Labels

Pinpoint

See product label—write responses to comprehension questions

Aim

To answer correctly 90% or more of the comprehension questions for each label

Feedback Device

The correct answers are provided on an answer card kept in a pocket attached to the back of the holder.

Materials

Manila folder with a label or wrapper (such as a food can label or a candy bar wrapper) attached to the front and comprehension questions concerning the label or wrapper written inside the folder; an answer key is placed in a library card pocket attached to the back of the folder

Pencil and paper

J. J. Foods	SOUP	Directions:
Ingredients	Tomato	
	12 oz.	

Outside

Directions
1. ⁓⁓ ⁓ ⁓⁓ ⁓
2. ⁓⁓⁓⁓ ⁓ ⁓ ⁓
Questions
1. What company makes the product?
2. What does the product weigh?
3. ⁓⁓⁓⁓
4. ⁓ ⁓⁓⁓
5. ⁓⁓ ⁓⁓
6. ⁓⁓ ⁓ ⁓⁓
7. ⁓⁓⁓
8. ⁓⁓ ⁓⁓⁓
9. ⁓⁓ ⁓ ⁓⁓
10. ⁓⁓ ⁓ ⁓⁓

Inside

Directions to the Learner

[Write inside the folder]

1 Read each comprehension question about the product label and write your answer on your own paper.

2 Check your answers with those on the answer card inside the pocket on the back of the folder. If they match, super work!

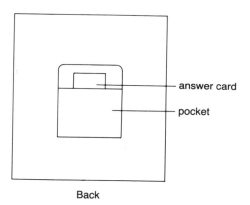

Back

Puzzles: Consonant-Vowel-Consonant Pattern

Pinpoint

See word—say word

Aim

To read 100 consonant-vowel-consonant pattern nouns in a 1-minute timing with two or fewer errors

Feedback Device

The two pieces of the heart puzzle fit together to indicate a correct match of word and picture.

Materials

Sets of heart puzzle pieces made from stiff paper or cardboard: one part of the heart contains a picture of a consonant-vowel-consonant word, and a second part fits together with the picture piece and has the word illustrated by the picture written on it

Index card with directions

Plastic sandwich bag to hold the puzzle pieces and directions

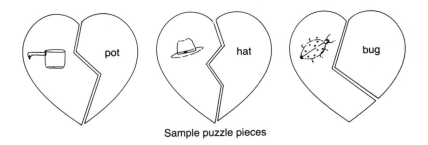

Sample puzzle pieces

Directions to the Learner

[Write on an index card and keep in the bag]
1. Sort all the pieces into two piles—words and pictures.
2. Read a word on a puzzle piece.
3. Find a picture piece showing that person, animal, or thing.
4. Check your answer by trying to fit the two pieces together to form a heart.
5. If the pieces fit together, great! If not, put the pieces back and try again later.

Suggestions to the Teacher

Let the students find their own pictures in old workbooks and magazines. Involve them in constructing the heart puzzles. Start with only five heart puzzles. For every five words the student can read to you, add five more. The goal is to read 100 words on the puzzle pieces in a 1-minute timing. Allow the students to practice with their bags of puzzle pieces at home.

Strips in a Folder: Following Written Directions

Pinpoint

See directions—draw design with three critical elements

Aim

To draw all of the designs correctly

Feedback Device

When the worksheet is pulled upward in the folder, the answers move into sight.

Materials

Manila folder with strips cut out across the front
Worksheet with directions to draw various designs and
    each design drawn under its directions
Pencil and paper

Directions to the Learner

[Write so they may be seen through the top opening]
1   Read the directions and draw the designs on
    your paper.

Directions:
1. ———————   3. ———————
2. ———————

1. Draw a square inside of a circle.
    ▣
2. Draw 6 stars across with dots
   in between.
    ★ • ★ • ★ • ★ • ★ • ★

Sample Worksheet

2 Pull the worksheet up to see drawings of the correct designs.

3 If your designs match the ones on the worksheet, good job!

Stylus: Fact or Opinion

Pinpoint

See sentence—insert stylus in correct answer hole to indicate if the sentence is fact or opinion

Aim

To identify correctly all the sentences as fact or opinion

Feedback Device

The student inserts the stylus in one of the answer holes to indicate his response. If his answer is correct, the task card can be removed from the box because the area below the correct answer is cut out and offers no resistance to the stylus.

Materials

Large cardboard or wooden box (see Poke Box in chapter 2 but make two evenly spaced holes across the front of the box)

Large rubber band

Stylus, pencil, or thin stick

Task cards with a sentence stating a fact or an opinion written at the top of the card and *fact* or *opinion* written above punched-out holes at the bottom of the card

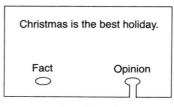

Sample card

Directions to the Learner

[Write on a card and keep with the deck]

1 Put the cards inside the rubber band in the box.

2 Read the sentence on the first card and decide if it is a fact or an opinion.

3 Poke the stick in the hole below your answer.

4 If you can easily pull the card from the box, congratulations! You picked the right answer.

5 Practice until you can identify all the sentences correctly. Then demonstrate this skill for the teacher.

Windows: Syllabication

Pinpoint

See word—write word showing syllables

Aim

To divide words into syllables correctly at the rate of 14 syllables per minute with one or no errors when given a probe sheet

Feedback Device

The correct answer is written after each word on the paper tape. The student turns the rollers to move the tape and the answers (written in a color) are revealed in a window in the box top.

Materials

Long, narrow box with a cardboard tube or wooden dowel at each end, with a piece of felt circling the rollers and lapping over and a window cut in the top of the box

Adding machine paper tape (same length as the felt) with a word written in black, and the number of syllables and the word divided into syllables written in a color below the word

Paper clips

Pencil and paper

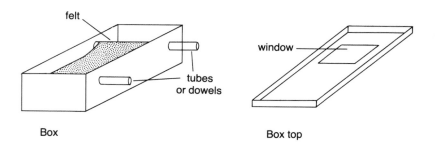

Box   Box top

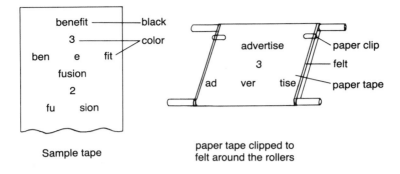

Sample tape

paper tape clipped to
felt around the rollers

Directions to the Learner

[Write on the tape]

1 Clip this tape on top of the felt strip and wind it tightly around the rollers.
2 Put the lid on the box and turn these directions to the window.
3 Turn the rollers and you will see a word written in black.
4 Write the word on your paper with spaces between the syllables.
5 If you want a hint, turn the rollers to see the number of syllables in the word.
6 Turn the rollers again to see the answer written in a color. If your answer matches, good thinking!

Suggestions to the Teacher

If may help the student further if syllabication rules are written on a card.

Reading Scope and Sequence Skills List*

Grade 1

Word Attack

        Relates spoken sounds to written symbols

        Recognizes all initial and final consonant sounds (single sounds and blends up to first vowel in word)

        Identifies likenesses and differences in sounds and structure of words

        Names the letter of the alphabet for single sounds he hears

        Recognizes short vowels in one-syllable words and substitutes different vowels to form new words *(bad:* substitute *e = bed)*

        Substitutes initial consonant to form new words

        Substitutes final consonant to form new words

        Recognizes long vowels in words ending in silent *e*

        Identifies rhyming words; decodes words with same phonogram/phonemic pattern *(at, cat, bat)*

        Recognizes endings: *s, es, ed, ing*

        Identifies compound words *(football)*

        Uses context clues to read words within his experience

Comprehension

        Relates printed words to objects or actions

        Follows printed directions *(Find the boy's house)*

        Reads to find information

        Draws conclusions from given facts *(What do you think happened then?)*

        Recalls main ideas of what has been read aloud

        Recalls details in story

        Arranges increasing numbers of events in sequence

        Uses pictures and context clues for meaning

        Makes comments and asks questions that indicate involvement with characters and story line

        Predicts events in a story

Source. From *Teaching Students with Learning Problems* by C. D. Mercer and A. R. Mercer. Columbus, Ohio: Charles E. Merrill, 1981, pp. 409–13. Reprinted by permission.

Relates causes and effects

Describes characters' feelings

Discusses feelings evoked by stories

Tells whether story is factual or fanciful (true-to-life or make-believe)

Grade 2

Word Attack

Produces the consonant blends in isolation: *bl, br, cl, cr, dr, dw, fr, fl, gl, gr, mp, nd, pl, pr, qu, sc, sl, st, str, sw, scr, sm, sn, sp, spl, squ, sk, spr, tr, tw, thr, -nt, -nk, -st*

Decodes words with consonant blends

Substitutes initial consonant blends to form other words

Identifies forms and sounds of consonant digraphs in initial position: *sh, ch, ph, th, wh*

Identifies forms and sounds of consonant digraphs in final position: *sh, ch, gh, ng, ph, th, sh*

Decodes four- and five-letter words that have regular short vowel sounds

Decodes words in which the vowels are long

Decodes words with final consonant blends

Decodes words ending in v–c plus silent *e (make, smoke, bone)*

Decodes consonant variants *(s—has, see; g—garden, large; c—music, ice)*

Decodes long *e* and *i* sound of *y*

Decodes vowel diphthongs: *oi, oy, ou, ow, ew*

Decodes words in which vowel is controlled by *r (far, fur, bar, more)*

Forms compound word with two known words *(baseball)*

Identifies root/base words in inflected forms of known words *(helpful, help; darkness, dark; unhappy, happy; recall, call)*

Decodes words in which final silent *e* is dropped before adding ending *(smoke, smoking)*

Identifies sounds and forms of consonant digraphs in medial position *(wishing)*

Decodes vowel digraphs/vowel teams: *oa, ai, ay, ee, ea, ie, ei*

Identifies sounds of *a* followed by *l, w,* or *u*

Decodes suffixes *(-less, -ful, -ness, -er, -est, -ly)*

Decodes prefixes *(un-, re-, dis-, pre-, pro-, ex-, en-)*

Identifies multiple sounds of long *a (ei, weigh; ai, straight; ay, day; ey, they)*

Decodes words with vowel digraph/vowel team irregularities *(bread, heart)*

Recognizes and knows meaning of contractions with one-letter omission

Identifies plural endings, irregular plurals, and *'s* possessive

Comprehension

Skims for information

Reads to answer questions *who, when, where, how,* and *what*

Makes judgments from given facts

Draws conclusions, answering such questions as "What do you think happened next?"

Begins to use contextual clues to determine meaning of a new word

Interprets simple figurative expressions

Interprets feelings of characters in stories

Recognizes the stereotyping of people in stories

Grade 3

Word Attack

Uses phonetic clues to recognize words

Identifies the beginning, middle, and end sounds of each word given orally

Recognizes silent vowels in words

Uses consonant digraphs as an aid to word attack

Identifies diphthongs *(ou, ow, oi, oy)* and pronounces words containing diphthongs

Knows when to double the final consonant before adding *-ing*

Uses vowel digraphs correctly

Reads unfamiliar words which contain *r*-controlled vowels

Reads root words and recognizes prefixes and suffixes *(-er, -est, -ing, -ed, -es, -ly, un-, re-, -less)*

Decodes silent *k* in *kn (know)*

Decodes silent *gh (though)*

Decodes words ending in *-ed (-ed, crooked; -t, looked)*

Decodes *dg (edge)*

Divides two-syllable words

Recognizes contractions

Recognizes the use of the apostrophe to show ownership

Hyphenates words using syllable rules

Recognizes the meanings of words used in different contexts

Selects the meaning which fits best according to the context in which the word is used

Comprehension

Finds main idea

Selects facts to support main idea

Draws logical conclusions

Reads for a definite purpose: to enjoy, to obtain answers, and to obtain a general idea of content

Recognizes shifts of meaning caused by using words in different context

Answers specific questions about material read

Follows written directions

Interprets descriptive words and phrases

Selects an appropriate title after reading an untitled selection

Composes his own questions about material read

Makes inferences about material read

Recognizes structure of plot (summarizes sequence of events)

Recognizes that characters change as a story develops

Identifies relationships among characters in a story

Compares similar elements in different stories

Grade 4

Word Attack

Uses phonetic clues to accent unfamiliar words correctly

Uses dictionary as an aid to attacking and pronouncing new words

Identifies and defines prefixes and suffixes

Reads synonyms, antonyms, and homonyms correctly at his reading level

Recognizes and uses words that signal relationships (*and, or, except, still, but, furthermore, especially, in this way, such as, on the other hand*)

Comprehension

Summarizes main ideas and selects facts to support main ideas

Identifies the subtopics of a selection

Finds factual and inferential information in answer to questions

Compares or contrasts selections

Compares information from different sources

Interprets literal and figurative language

Selects the meaning of a specific word when the meaning is implied but not stated

Predicts possible endings based on previous events in an unfinished selection

Recognizes theme of story

Describes times, place, characters, and sequence of action in a story

Grade 5

Word Attack

Applies phonetic principles and structural analysis skills in combination with context clues to read unfamiliar words

Uses context clues to derive meaning from unfamiliar words

Uses phonetic clues to accent unfamiliar words correctly

Comprehension

Investigates facts

Identifies and recalls story facts and significant details

Infers a character's appearance, moods, feelings, traits, and motives

Recognizes large thought division within an expository work including parts, chapters, sections, acts, and scenes

Distinguishes between good and poor summaries

Identifies the point of view in a selection

Analyzes a story in terms of who acted, what action was taken, and what resulted from the action

Cites examples of one good and one bad quality of a character treated in a biography

Recognizes structure of plot and identifies conflict or problems

Identifies influence of setting on characters and events

Grade 6

Word Attack

Uses a repertoire of word attack skills

Uses root words, prefixes, and suffixes to derive the meaning of words

Comprehension

Compares reading selections as to suitability for a given purpose (dramatization, reading to others, inclusion in a bibliography)

Recognizes elements of characterization (presentation of the characters, completeness of characters, function of the characters, and relationships with other characters)

Recognizes transitional paragraphs that connect chapters, sections, and episodes

Proves a point with factual information from the reading selections

Interprets colloquial and figurative expressions

Describes the rising action, climax, and falling action in a story

Summarizes the main conflict in a story, giving the underlying causes of the conflict and the events that contributed to the conflict

Identifies the mood of a selection and the words or phrases that establish the mood

Identifies the basic elements of a news story *(who, what, where, when, why, and how)*

Analyzes and describes the point of view in an editorial

6

SPELLING MATERIALS

This chapter illustrates how self-correcting materials may be adapted for spelling instruction. A spelling scope and sequence skills network, provided at the end of this chapter, will assist the teacher in selecting target skills for individual learners. The network includes skills that focus on consonants, vowels, morphemes, recall devices, special words, and dictionary skills for grades one through seven.

Answer on Back: Body Part Names

Pinpoint

See picture of body part—write name

Aim

To name and spell correctly 12 different body parts during a mastery test

Feedback Device

The correct name and spelling are provided on the back of the card illustrating the word.

Materials

Twelve 3″ x 5″ index cards with illustrations of different body parts on one side and the name of the body part on the reverse side
Pencil and paper

Directions to the Learner

1 Sort the cards with the picture side face up.
2 On your own paper, write the name of the body part shown.
3 Check your answer by looking on the back of the card.
4 When you can do all 12 cards, you are ready to take the mastery test. I know you can pass it on your first try!

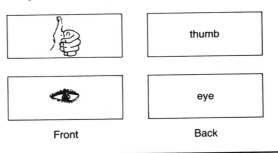

Front   Back

Cassette: Diphthongs "oi" and "oy"

Pinpoint

Hear word—write word

Aim

To spell correctly all words presented on a tape at the rate of approximately 50 letters per minute during a spelling quiz

Feedback Device

Following the spelling activity presented on the tape, the correct answers are given on the tape.

Materials

Cassette tape recorder
Cassette tape prepared with spelling words that contain
    the diphthongs *oi* and *oy* (for example, royal, boiling,
    soil, toyed, foil); correct spellings follow at the end of
    the tape
Pencil and paper

Directions to the Learner

[Record on the tape]
1 Get your pencil and paper ready. You will hear words that contain the diphthongs *oi* and *oy.*
2 Write every word you can.
3 Check your spellings with those given at the end of the tape.
4 Practice until you can keep pace with the tape and spell all the words correctly. Then you are ready for your spelling quiz.

Colored Acetate Folder: Months of the Year

Pinpoint

See incomplete word—fill in the missing letters

Aim

To spell the months of the year in sequence with 100% accuracy when given the first letter of each word

Feedback Device

After writing his answers, the student opens the folder to see the correct answers written in yellow.

Materials

Colored acetate folder (red is best)

Separate worksheet for each month, showing incomplete spellings of the name of the month in black and blanks filled in with yellow marker

Final worksheet containing an incomplete spelling of each month

Grease pencil or washable acetate marker

Damp paper towel

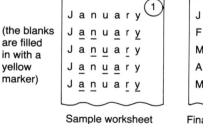

(the blanks are filled in with a yellow marker)

Sample worksheet   Final worksheet format

Directions to the Learner

1 Put the worksheets in order from 1 to 13.
2 Place the worksheets in the colored folder.
3 Using the grease pencil, trace over the letters in the first line.
4 Finish the rest of the lines by tracing over the letters you are given and filling in the blanks.
5 Check your work by pulling the worksheet out and matching the black and yellow letters with what you wrote.
6 Use a damp paper towel to clean the plastic and then do the next worksheet.
7 If you can do the last worksheet—good job! Now you can spell all the months of the year.

Flap: Consonant-Vowel-Consonant Pattern

Pinpoint

See picture—write consonant-vowel-consonant word

Aim

To spell correctly 20 consonant-vowel-consonant words during a word game with three other students

Feedback Device

A flap is located on the poster board. When the flap is raised, the answer is revealed.

Materials

Round disc of poster board (approximately 10″ in diameter) divided into several sections, each with a word written near its outside edge and a picture illustrating the word in the portion of the section closest to the center of the circle; the round disc is attached to the back of a square piece of poster board (approximately 11″ x 11″) with a brass fastener, with a small window

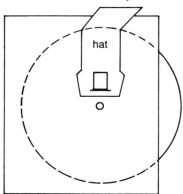
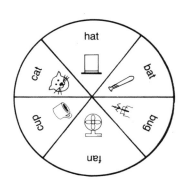

Sample disc

cut out at the top to reveal the top portion of the disc
and a larger window below it to reveal the lower portion
of the disc; a flexible flap (such as vinyl wallpaper) is
placed over the top window
Pencil and paper

Directions to the Learner

1   Turn the spinner wheel until you see a picture
    in the window.
2   Write the word for the picture on your paper.
3   Lift the flap to see the correct spelling of the
    word.
4   Check the correct spelling with the word on
    your paper.
5   Try to do the whole wheel without making any
    mistakes.
6   Now you're ready to play the board game with
    three other players. Good luck!

Suggestions to the Teacher

To avoid confusion, be sure only one item is in the illustration
and that the word list does not include synonyms.

Holes: Sight Words

Pinpoint

See incorrectly spelled sight word—detect extra letter

Aim

To find unnecessary letters in the sight words on the cards with 100% accuracy

Feedback Device

A golf tee is inserted in the hole underneath an incorrect letter in a word. If the choice is correct, the tee will appear through the hole circled in green on the back of the card.

Materials

Index cards with a word containing an extra letter and a reinforced hole punched out below each letter; on the back, the hole indicating the correct answer is circled in green
Golf tee
Pencil and paper

Directions to the Learner

[Write on the top card of the deck]
    1 Sort the cards so the words face up.

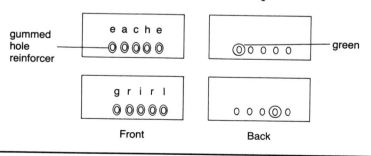

Front   Back

2 Notice that each word contains an extra letter and is not spelled correctly.

3 Find the extra letter and put the golf tee through the hole underneath it.

4 To check your answer, look on the back of the card. If you are right, the tee is through the green hole.

5 Practice until you can choose all of the correct answers.

6 On your paper, make a list of the proper spelling of each word and show your super work to the teacher. She'll be proud of you!

Light: Homonyms

Pinpoint

See incomplete sentence and two homonyms—select the correct homonym

Aim

To select the correct homonym on at least 18 out of 20 cards in a demonstration for a classmate

Feedback Device

When the correct answer is selected with the stylus, an electrical connection is completed and a light comes on.

Materials

Electric Learning Board (see chapter 2 for a list of materials and construction guidelines)

5" x 8" stimulus cards prepared with an incomplete sentence and two homonym answer choices

Directions to the Learner

1   Place a card on the board by lining up the arrow on the card with the arrow on the board.

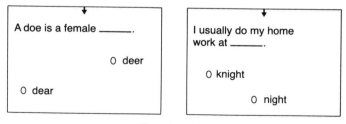

Sample cards

2 Read the sentence and select the correct homonym by putting the stylus in the hole next to your answer choice.

3 If your choice is correct, the light will come on.

4 When you can do all the cards without a mistake, demonstrate how much you know to a classmate.

Matching: Color Names

Pinpoint

See colored shape and letter cards—arrange letters to spell the color's name

Aim

To spell correctly 10 color names in a demonstration for a classmate

Feedback Device

When the letters are arranged in the correct order and then turned over, a picture is formed.

Materials

Ten 4″ x 6″ index cards which are cut in pieces (one letter on each piece) after the name of a color is written on the front and a picture is pasted on the back

Ten small envelopes, each of which contains the letter cards to a color and has the color drawn on the front of the envelope

Large envelope

Directions to the Learner

[Write on the outside of the large envelope]

1. Take one small envelope out of this envelope.
2. Look at the color on the outside of the small envelope.

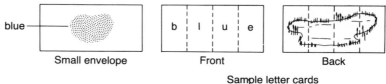

blue		
Small envelope	Front	Back

Sample letter cards

3 Take the cards out of the envelope and put them letter-side up.

4 Put the letters in the order that spells the name of the color.

5 To check your answer, turn the cards over in reverse order: turn the last card over and place it under the first card, then turn the next to last card over and place it under the second card, etc. If you spelled the color right, the backs of the cards show a picture.

6 When you can do all 10 color names, show your new skill to a classmate. Great work!

Pockets: Silent "e" Pattern

Pinpoint

See crossword puzzle clue—write word containing silent *e* in puzzle

Aim

To complete correctly a crossword puzzle involving silent *e* words

Feedback Device

The solution to the puzzle is contained in a pocket on the back of the puzzle card. Also, the puzzle itself provides some feedback.

Materials

Laminated piece of tagboard, 12" x 12", showing a cross-word puzzle and clues for the silent *e* words (for example, a dog eats it—*bone;* a clock tells it—*time*); an answer sheet is placed in a library card pocket attached to the back of the puzzle card
Grease pencil or washable acetate marker

Directions to the Learner

1   Read a clue and think of a "magic *e*" word that will fit in the blanks.

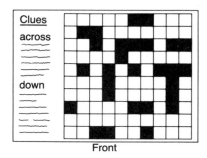

Front

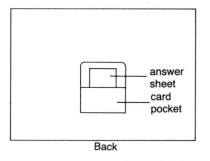

Back

2 Using the grease pencil, write your answer in the puzzle.

3 When you have finished the puzzle, check your work with the answer sheet in the pocket on the back of the puzzle.

Puzzles: Plurals

Pinpoint

See root words—write plurals that require adding *s* or *es*

Aim

To write the correct plural form of all the words

Feedback Device

After looking at the puzzle pieces with root words and writing the plural form for each word, the student completes the two-piece puzzles, revealing the correct plural form.

Materials

Laminated tagboard or cardboard cut into two irregular pieces with one piece showing the root word in red letters and the corresponding piece showing the appropriate plural ending in blue letters
Plastic sandwich bag to store puzzle pieces
Pencil and paper

Directions to the Learner

1 Sort all the puzzle pieces into two piles according to red letters and blue letters.
2 Look at the cards with red letters. These are root words.

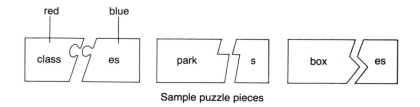

Sample puzzle pieces

3 On your paper, write the plural form of the root word.

4 After you have completed the red pile, find the blue puzzle piece that fits each red piece.

5 Check the finished puzzles with the words on your paper.

Strips in a Folder: Prefixes

Pinpoint

See meaning—write prefix

Aim

To spell the prefixes on a mastery test with 90% accuracy

Feedback Device

After writing the answers with a grease pencil on the strips cut in the laminated folder, the student moves the worksheet upward to reveal the correct answers.

Materials

Laminated manila folder with strips cut out across the front

Grease pencil or washable acetate marker

Worksheet with a word in black giving the meaning of a prefix and the corresponding prefix in blue underneath its meaning

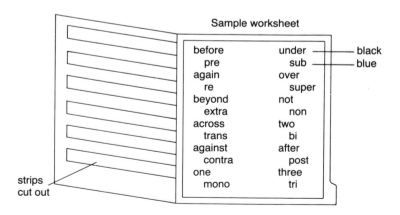

Sample worksheet

before	under	black
pre	sub	blue
again	over	
re	super	
beyond	not	
extra	non	
across	two	
trans	bi	
against	after	
contra	post	
one	three	
mono	tri	

strips cut out

Directions to the Learner

1 Insert the worksheet so only the words written in black are visible.

2 Using the grease pencil, write under each meaning the prefix that corresponds.

3 When you have finished, pull the worksheet up to reveal the prefixes written in blue. Check your answers with the worksheet.

4 When you are ready, turn in the worksheet and take the mastery test.

Stylus: Abbreviations

Pinpoint

See word—select correct abbreviation

Aim

To select the correct abbreviation with 100% accuracy for all the words in a demonstration for the teacher

Feedback Device

The student places a stylus in the hole to indicate his response. If the correct answer is selected, the card can be pulled out of the box with ease.

Materials

Cardboard or wooden box large enough to hold index cards (see Poke Box in chapter 2)
Large rubber band
Stylus, pencil, or thin stick
Index cards with a word written at the top of each card and three possible abbreviations written above punched out holes at the bottom of each card

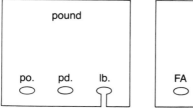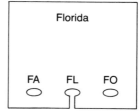

Sample cards

Directions to the Learner

[Write on the top card of the deck]

1 Place the cards behind the rubber band in the box. Be sure the printed sides face the side of the box that has holes punched in it.
2 Read the word at the top of the card.
3 Choose the correct abbreviation by poking the stylus in the hole under your choice. If your answer is right, you can pull the card gently out of the box.
4 Practice until you can answer each card correctly on the first try. Then demonstrate what you have learned to the teacher.

Windows: Inflected Forms of Words Ending in "y"

Pinpoint

See word and ending—write correct inflected form

Aim

To demonstrate for the classroom aide the ability to write with 90% accuracy the inflected forms of the words ending in *y*

Feedback Device

After a response is written, the tab is pulled upward to reveal the correct answer in the window.

Materials

10" x 5" piece of cardboard with a window cut in the top and two large rubber bands across the back and knotted in the front

11" x 3" strips of tagboard each with a direction written at the top, a list of words written in blue, and the inflected form of each word written in red under each word

Pencil and paper

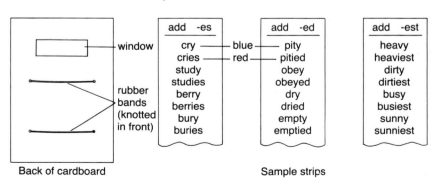

add -es	add -ed	add -est
cry —— blue	pity	heavy
cries —— red	pitied	heaviest
study	obey	dirty
studies	obeyed	dirtiest
berry	dry	busy
berries	dried	busiest
bury	empty	sunny
buries	emptied	sunniest

Back of cardboard

Sample strips

Directions to the Learner

1 Slide the strip underneath the rubber bands so the first blue word appears in the window.

2 Follow the directions written at the top of the strip and write your answer on your own paper.

3 Pull the strip upward until the next word (in red) appears in the window. This is the correct answer. Check it with your work.

4 When you can complete all the words correctly, show the classroom aide what you have learned. You should feel good about mastering this skill!

Spelling Scope and Sequence Skills List*

Many spelling skills are repeated at each grade level. However, the level of difficulty of the words to which the spelling skill applies increases with each grade level. A bullet (•) denotes the initial use of a specific skill.

Grade 1

- Spells two- and three-letter words
- Spells own first and last name correctly

Grade 2

Spells consonant sounds correctly:
- regular consonants *(bed, hat, sun, yes)*
- *sh, ch, ng, wh,* and *th (fish, much, sing, which, this, with)*
- *x* spelling of *ks (box, fox)*
- *c* spelling of *k (cold)*
- *c* and *k (cat, kept)*
- *ck (duck, black)*
- *s* spelling of *s* and *z (sun, as)*
- consonant blends *(flag)*
- silent consonants *(doll, hill, who, know, would)*

Spells vowel sounds correctly:
- short vowel sound in initial or medial position *(am, did)*
- long vowel spelled by a single vowel *(go, be)*
- two vowels together *(meat, rain)*
- vowel-consonant-silent *e (home, ride)*
- *ow* spelling of long *o (snow, grow)*
- *ay* spelling of long *a (day, play)*
- final *y* spelling of long *e (baby, very)*
- final *y* spelling of long *i (my, why)*

Source: From *Teaching Students with Learning Problems* by C. D. Mercer and A. R. Mercer. Columbus, Ohio: Charles E. Merrill, 1981, pp. 414–20. Reprinted by permission.

- *oo* spelling of *u̇* and *ü* *(good, soon)*
- *ow* and *ou* spellings of the *ou* sound in *owl* and *mouse* *(down, house)*
- *oy* spelling of the *oi* sound *(boy, toy)*
- vowel sounds before *r*
- the *er* spelling of *r* at the end *(over, teacher)*
- *er, ir, or,* and *ur* spellings of *er (her, bird, work, hurt)*
- the *or* and *ar* spelling of *ôr (for)*
- the *ar* spelling of *är (car)*
- unexpected single vowel spellings *(from, off, cold)*
- unexpected vowel-consonant-silent *e (give, done)*
- unexpected spellings with two vowels together *(been, said)*
- other unexpected vowel spellings *(they, are)*

Uses morphemes to make structural changes:
- *s* plural *(cats, cows)*
- *s* or *es* for third person singular *(live, lives)*
- *s* to show possession *(yours, ours)*
- *d* or *ed* ending for past tense *(played)*
- *ing* ending *(blowing)*
- *er* noun agent ending *(singer, player)*
- *er* and *est* endings *(old, older, oldest)*

Uses devices to aid spelling recall:
- syllabication *(yel low, go ing)*
- recognizing compounds *(today)*
- recognizing rhyming words *(pet, get)*

Spells selected words correctly:
- simple homonyms *(to, two, too)*

Grade 3

Spells consonant sounds correctly:

    regular consonants *(must, trip, ask, zoo)*

    sh, ch, ng, wh, and *th (shoe, child, sang, while, those, thank)*
- *nk (drunk, drank)*
- *x (next)*

    c spelling of *k (cup)*

    c and *k (ask, cake)*

    ck (chicken, clock)

    s spelling of *s* and *z (gas, has)*
- *gh* spelling of *f (laugh)*

consonant blends *(twin)*

silent consonants *(bell, grass, walk, catch, wrote, night)*

Spells vowel sounds correctly:

short vowel in initial or medial position *(bad, send, stop)*

long vowel

- single vowel in open syllables *(paper, table)*

two vowels together *(soap, cream, train)*

vowel-consonant-silent *e (game, side, snake)*

ow spelling of long *o (window)*

ay spelling of long *a (always, yesterday)*

final *y* spelling of long *e (city, study, sorry)*

final *y* spelling of long *i (cry, try)*

oo spelling of *ü* and *ü (cook, shoot)*

ow and *ou* spellings of the *ou* sound in *owl* and *mouse (flower, ground)*

vowel sounds before *r*

- the *er* spelling of *ər* at the end *(ever, another)*
- the *or* spelling of *ər* at the end *(color)*

er, ir, or, and ur spellings of *er (person, third, word, turning)*

the *or* and *ar* spelling of *ôr (horse, warm)*

the *ar* spelling of *är (star, party)*

unexpected single vowels *(kind, full, cost)*

unexpected vowel-consonant-silent *e (whose, sure)*

unexpected spellings with two vowels together *(bread, great, friend)*

other unexpected vowel spellings *(aunt, says, could)*

- *le* spelling of the *əl* sound *(people, table)*

Uses morphemes to make structural changes:

- *s* or *es* plural *(cups, buses, dishes)*
- changing *y* to *i* before *es (cry, cries)*

s or *es* for third person singular *(jumps, races, misses)*

d or *ed* ending for past tense *(asked, laughed)*

ing ending *(reading, thinking)*

- *ing* ending with doubled consonant *(clapping, beginning)*
- *ing* ending with dropped silent *e (skating, moving)*

er noun agent ending *(painter, builder)*

er and *est* endings *(high, higher, highest)*

Uses devices to aid spelling recall:

syllabication *(bas ket, ta ble)*

recognizing compounds (airplane, something)
recognizing rhyming words (hand, land)
Spells selected words correctly:
homonyms (it, it's; eight, ate)
Uses dictionary skills:
- alphabetizing—sequencing of words in alphabetical order

Grade 4

Spells consonant phonemes correctly:
sh, ch, and ng (ship, rich, hang)
- voiced and unvoiced th (bath, those)
- ch spelling of k (schoolhouse)
- wh spelling of hw (wheel)
- g spelling of g or j (frog, bridge)
- c spelling of k or s (cage, circus)
- ck spelling of k (luck)
- x spelling of ks (fix)
- qu spelling of kw (queen)
- nk spelling of ngk (monkey)
- ph spelling of f (elephant)
consonant blends (brain)
silent consonants (answer)
Spells vowel phonemes correctly:
short medial vowel (cap)
long sound spelled with vowel-consonant-silent e (bone)
long sound spelled with two vowels (tie)
long sound spelled in open syllables (hotel)
vowels before r (fur, born)
ou and ow spellings of ou (count, cowboy)
- ow spelling of the ö sound (unknown)
oo spelling of the u and ü sounds (hook, stood)
- oi and oy spellings of oi (noise, enjoy)
- o, al, au, and aw spellings of ô (north, tall)
- əl and l (castle, jungle)
- y spelling of ē (busy)
Uses morphemes to make structural changes:
d and ed ending (recalled, untied)
s and es ending (socks, chimneys, churches)
- irregular plurals (feet)

doubling a final consonant before *ing (stepping)*

dropping final silent *e* before *ing (trading)*

er and *est* endings *(paler, palest)*

- *ly* ending *(finally)*

changing of *y* to *i* before *es (bodies)*

ing ending *(interesting)*

- number suffixes *(fifteen, fifty)*
- suffixes to change part of speech *(kindness, playful, friendly)*
- prefixes to change meaning *(unlock, exchange, re-place, promote)*

Uses devices to aid spelling recall:

syllable divisions *(bot tom, ho tel, cab in)*

- unexpected spellings *(minute)*

compounds *(upstairs, watermelon)*

Spells selected words:

homonyms *(whole, hymn)*

- contractions *(aren't)*
- months *(February)*

Uses dictionary skills:

- using guide words—recognition of words grouped by alphabetical similarities

Grade 5

Spells consonant phonemes correctly:

sh, ch, and *ng (shade, chest, among)*

voiced and unvoiced *th (sixth, either)*

ch spelling of *k (echo)*

wh spelling of *hw (whistle)*

g spelling of *g* or *j (gate, damage)*

c spelling of *k* or *s (cook, princess)*

ck spelling of *k (attack)*

x spelling of *ks (expect)*

qu spelling of *kw (quarter)*

nk spelling of *ngk (trunk)*

silent consonants *(ghost)*

Spells vowel phonemes correctly:

short medial vowels *(bunch)*

vowel-consonant-silent *e (prize)*

various spellings before *r (term, artist)*

ou and *ow* spellings of *ou (outfit, shower)*

- *ow* spelling of *ō (crow)*

  oo spelling of the *ŭ* and *ü* sounds *(loose, choosing)*

  oi and *oy* spellings of *oi (join, voice)*

  o, al, au, and *aw* spellings of *ô (crawl, chalk)*
- spellings of *el* and *l (model, central)*

  y spelling of *ē (worry, crazy)*

Uses morphemes to make structural changes:

  d or *ed* ending *(excited, earned)*

  s or *es* ending *(beads, beaches)*

  doubling final consonant before *ing (chopping, snapping)*

  dropping final silent *e* before *ing (ruling, shaking)*

  number suffixes *(thirteen, sixty)*

Spells selected words:

  contractions *(they're)*

Uses dictionary skills:
- locating words in a dictionary—ability to find words of uncertain spelling in a dictionary

Grade 6

Spells consonant phonemes correctly:

  sh, ch, and *ng* consonants *(shelf, chain, gang)*

  voiced and unvoiced *th (thread, leather)*

  ch spelling of *k (orchestra)*

  wh spelling of *hw (whale)*

  g spelling of *g* or *j (cigar, pledge)*

  c spelling of *k* or *s (cabbage, voice)*

  ck spelling of *k (ticket)*

  x spelling of *ks (expedition)*

  qu spelling of *kw (acquaint)*

  nk spelling of *ngk (plank)*
- *ph* spelling of *f (alphabet)*

Spells vowel phonemes correctly:

  long sound with two vowels *(coach)*

  long sound in open syllables *(soda)*

  various spellings before *r (stairs, skirt)*

  ou and *ow* spellings of *ou (growl, surround)*

  ow spelling of *ō (narrow)*

  oo spelling of *ŭ* and *ü (bloom, shook)*

  oi and *oy* spellings of *oi (spoil, voyage)*

o, al, au, and *aw* spelling of *ô (author, naughty)*

*ə*l and *l* sounds *(carnival, barrel)*

Uses morphemes to make structural changes:

        changing of *y* to *i* before *es (pantries, colonies)*

- forming plurals of nouns which end in *o (pianos, potatoes)*

        ing ending *(stretching)*

        er and *est* endings *(tinier, tiniest)*

        ly ending *(dreadfully, especially)*

        suffixes and prefixes *(harmless, attractive, dishonest, incorrect)*

        d or *ed* ending *(continued, contracted)*

        s or *es* ending *(insects, sandwiches)*

        irregular plurals *(calves, geese)*

Uses dictionary skills:

- locating appropriate word meaning—awareness and selection of multiple word meanings and appropriate word usage

Grades 7 and above

Spells selected words:

- hyphenated words *(tongue-tied)*
  silent letters—*b, h, m, g, p (pneumonia)*
- letter combinations: *-ient, -ian, -ium, -iasm, -iable, -ure (transient, enthusiasm)*
- word endings: *-ance, -ence, -ense, -ogy, -cede, -ceed (biology, ignorance)*

Uses dictionary skills:

- understanding pronunciation marks—ability to interpret diacritical markings

7

MATERIALS
FOR WRITTEN
EXPRESSION

This chapter shows how self-correcting materials may be used to teach a variety of handwriting and written expression skills. A handwriting scope and sequence skills network and a written expression scope and sequence skills network, included at the end of this chapter, will assist the teacher in selecting and adapting target skills for individual learners. The handwriting network presents handwriting skills emphasized in kindergarten through grade six. The written expression network includes capitalization, punctuation, written composition, and creative expression skills for students in kindergarten through grade six.

Answer on Back: Irregular Past-Tense Verbs

Pinpoint

See verb—write past-tense form

Aim

To write the correct irregular past-tense form of 15 verbs on a mastery test

Feedback Device

The correct past-tense form of the verb is written in a contrasting color on the reverse side of the card.

Materials

15 index cards with the present tense of the verb written in black on one side of the card and the past tense of the verb written in blue on the reverse side
Pencil and paper

Directions to the Learner

[Write on the top card of the deck]
1 Sort the cards so that the black writing is face up.

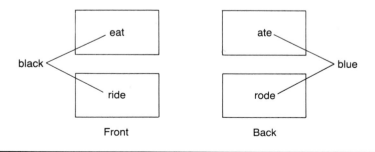

2 Read the first card and write on your paper the past tense for the verb. Use the singular form. *Warning:* These verbs are irregular! Adding *ed* as we usually do will result in some strange words and wrong answers. It may help you to put the words in sentences: Today I _____, but yesterday I _____.

3 Check your answer by looking at the word written in blue on the back of the card.

4 When you can give the past tense of all 15 verbs correctly, ask the teacher for the mastery test. It has the same verbs on it, so this practice should give you a great chance of getting a perfect score. Good luck!

Cassette: Punctuation From Intonation

Pinpoint

See and hear text—write punctuation where necessary

Aim

To write correctly 90% of the punctuation marks in a text after hearing the text read on a cassette tape

Feedback Device

Following the oral presentation of the text on the cassette tape, the same text is presented again with the necessary punctuation marks specified.

Materials

Cassette tape recorder

Cassette tape prepared with a reading passage at the learner's reading level in which the speaker is careful to convey all necessary pauses and intonations that indicate punctuation marks; following the first presentation, the same reading passage is presented with the necessary punctuation marks specified

Typed copy of the reading passage written in capital letters and without punctuation which is attached to a piece of tagboard and laminated

Grease pencil or washable acetate marker

tagboard

Story #7

MOUNTAIN CLIMBING IS A DANGEROUS
BUT EXCITING SPORT CLIMBERS MUST
ANTICIPATE DIFFICULTIES AND THEY
MUST PREPARE THEIR MINDS BODIES
AND EQUIPMENT FOR ALL CONDITIONS

Sample text

Directions to the Learner

1   Get the typed copy of Story #7 and a washable acetate marker or a grease pencil. The speaker will read Story #7 and your job is to listen for clues about where punctuation is needed. Punctuation is a way for writers to show what their words would sound like if said naturally.

2   Listen carefully for every hint the speaker's voice gives you about necessary punctuation. When you hear a short pause, write a comma. Longer pauses call for a period. If the speaker shows strong, excited emotion, then the sentence should end with an exclamation mark. If you hear the speaker's voice go "up" at the end of a sentence, you will need a question mark. Also, watch for possessive nouns and contractions that need apostrophes.

3   Using the grease pencil, write the marks on the typed copy of the story. The story needs 20 punctuation marks. Rewind the tape and listen to the passage as many times as you like.

4   After you have finished, listen to the second part of the tape. This time the speaker will tell you where punctuation is needed. Check your work. Your goal is to get 18 of the 20 punctuation marks the story needs in the right places.

5   If you missed more than two marks, wipe off your first marks and listen to the first part of the tape again during your writing time tomorrow. If you missed two or fewer marks, congratulations! You may mark the story off on your progress chart and tomorrow you may try Story #8.

Colored Acetate Folder: Cursive Writing

Pinpoint

See arrows and series of dots—write cursive letters

Aim

To complete cursive letters by following the arrows and series of dots provided

Feedback Device

The completed letters are written on the black dots with a yellow felt-tip pen. The colored acetate folder conceals the yellow letters until the learner removes the worksheet from the folder.

Materials

Colored (red) acetate folder with binder
Grease pencil or washable acetate marker
Worksheet prepared with black arrows to indicate the starting point of writing the letter and black dots indicating the letter form; the completed letter is written over the black dots with a yellow felt-tip pen

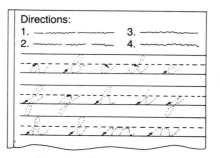

Sample worksheet inside folder

Directions to the Learner

[Write at the top of the worksheet]

1 Use an acetate marker or grease pencil to write on the plastic folder.

2 Follow the arrows and dots to make the cursive letters.

3 Pull the worksheet out of the folder when you have finished and compare your work with the yellow letters. With practice, you will be writing cursive soon!

Suggestions to the Teacher

The dots can be faded gradually, providing fewer and fewer clues about the shape of the letters. Also, a second worksheet written in dark ink showing examples of the letters that correspond to the dots may be kept in the folder. This may be placed under the learner's marks on the acetate to compare form.

Flap: Complete Versus Incomplete Sentences

Pinpoint

See word group—say whether sentence is complete or incomplete

Aim

To identify correctly all the word groups as either complete or incomplete sentences in an oral demonstration for a peer tutor

Feedback Device

After the learner makes a response, he raises a flap to reveal the correct answer.

Materials

Cardboard box (approximately 4″ square) cut as illustrated, with a piece of felt (approximately 2″ x 2″) stapled over a hole in the front of the box

4″ x 6″ index cards prepared with a group of words in sentence form at the top of the card and the word *complete* or *incomplete* written at the bottom of the card so it will show through the hole cut in the box

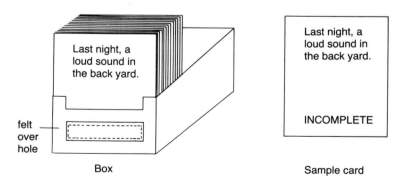

Box   Sample card

Directions to the Learner

[Write on the top index card of the deck]

1 Notice that each card in the box shows a group of words. Some are complete sentences; some are incomplete sentences.

2 Look at the first card and decide if the words form a complete or incomplete sentence. Say your answer to yourself.

3 Check your response by raising the flap and looking at the answer. Then move that card to the back of the box and try the next card.

4 Try to reach the goal of getting all the cards right on your first try. Practice will get you there.

5 When you have reached your goal, show off to a peer tutor. Great work!

Holes: Dictionary Skills

Pinpoint

See word—locate the word in the dictionary and write the number of the page where it was found

Aim

To locate vocabulary words in a dictionary and write the correct page number on which each word appears

Feedback Device

The student places a piece of paper under the tagboard material and writes his page number answers in the holes of the material. The correct page numbers are written on the back of the material next to the appropriate hole. When the student turns over the material and lines up the holes with his responses, the page numbers should match.

Materials

Piece of tagboard with holes cut down the center of the material and a word written next to each hole; on the back of the material, the appropriate page number is written next to each hole

Dictionary

Pencil and paper

Directions:
1. ___ ___ ___ ___
2. ___ ___ ___
3. ___ ___ ___
Words for "feeling good"

[ ] joyful

content [ ]

[ ] pleased

Page numbers in Dictionary

[ ] 459

180 [ ]

[ ] 650

Front   Back

172

Directions to the Learner

[Write at the top of the material]

1 Put a piece of paper under this cardboard so that the paper appears in every hole.

2 Look up each word in your dictionary. Write the number of the page you find it on in the hole next to the word on the cardboard.

3 When you have finished, turn over this cardboard and line up the holes with your page numbers. If you found each word correctly, the numbers written next to each hole will match yours exactly.

Light: Capitalization

Pinpoint

See sentence without capitalization—indicate the proper nouns that need capital letters

Aim

To identify correctly in a demonstration for the teacher all the proper nouns that need to be capitalized

Feedback Device

When the student places a stylus in a hole under the first letter of a proper noun, a light comes on to indicate that a correct choice has been made.

Materials

Electric Learning Board (see chapter 2 for a list of materials and construction guidelines)

5″ x 8″ stimulus cards showing a sentence without capitalization

Directions to the Learner

[Write on the cover card of the deck]

1   Place a card on the Electric Learning Board by lining up the arrow on the card with the arrow on the board.

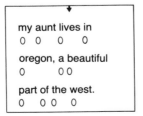 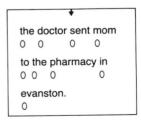

Sample cards

174

2 Read the sentence and decide which words are proper nouns that should be capitalized.

3 Place the stylus in the hole under the word(s) you think should be capitalized. If you are right, the light will come on.

4 When you can complete the entire set of cards and find 30 proper nouns without any second tries, show the teacher your success at this skill.

Suggestions to the Teacher

It is easier to construct these cards if the holes are punched first for the correct answers (according to the wiring system) and the proper nouns are written above them. Then write the rest of the sentence around the proper nouns and punch holes that do not correspond with those wired to complete the circuit.

Matching: Subject and Predicate

Pinpoint

See sentence—point to the space between the subject and the predicate

Aim

To identify correctly the division between subjects and predicates in all of the sentences in a demonstration for the classroom aide

Feedback Device

When the student matches the correct arrow card with the sentence card, a picture is formed on the reverse side of the two cards.

Materials

Index cards which are cut in two pieces lengthwise after a sentence is written on the top and an arrow pointing to the division between the subject and predicate is drawn on the bottom; a picture is pasted on the back of each card before it is cut

Plastic sandwich bag to hold the card pieces

Directions to the Learner

[Write on an index card kept in the bag]
  1 Sort the cards into two sets, sentences and arrows.
  2 Read a sentence and decide where the subject ends and the predicate begins.

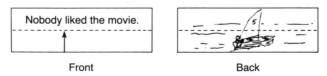

Front   Back

---

3 Find an arrow card that will point to this space when the edges of both cards are lined up.

4 To see if you are right, turn over both cards. If they make a complete picture, you are right. Congratulations!

5 If the two cards do not make a picture, turn them back over and try another arrow card.

6 Practice until you can get all the cards right on the first try. Now you are ready to demonstrate this skill to the classroom aide. Good for you!

Suggestions to the Teacher

Typing the cards allows you to use longer, more complex sentences. Be sure that all the sentences divide in different places on the cards, so that only one arrow card will provide the correct match.

Pockets: Proofreading

Pinpoint

See text with spelling and punctuation errors—mark appropriate corrections

Aim

To proofread the paragraphs with spelling and punctuation errors and mark all the appropriate corrections

Feedback Device

A second copy of the paragraphs with all the corrections marked is folded and kept in a pocket attached to the back of the material.

Materials

Laminated piece of tagboard containing paragraphs with spelling and punctuation errors; answer key showing the paragraphs with correct spelling and punctuation is placed in a pocket attached to the back

Grease pencil or washable acetate marker

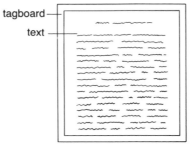
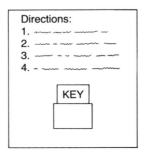

Front   Back

Directions to the Learner

[Write on the back of the material]

1. Pretend you are a proofreader for a popular magazine. One of your writers gave you this story for next week's issue. You have to be sure the story is perfect before it goes to the typesetter.

2. Read the story on the other side of this board and find all the punctuation and spelling errors.

3. Correct the errors using an acetate marker.

4. To see if you caught all the errors, look at the answer key in the pocket on the back. If you missed any mistakes, wipe off the first set of corrections and try again. Proofreaders have to catch *all* the mistakes writers make.

Puzzles: Plural Versus Possessive Forms of Nouns

Pinpoint

See descriptive phrase—write correct plural or possessive form of the noun

Aim

To write with 90% accuracy the correct plural or possessive noun form that corresponds to a descriptive phrase, in a demonstration for a peer tutor

Feedback Device

After the learner writes his responses, he fits the two-piece puzzles together to reveal the correct answers.

Materials

Strips of cardboard cut into two puzzle pieces with one piece showing a descriptive phrase written in red and the corresponding piece giving the correct plural or possessive noun form written in black
Plastic sandwich bag to store puzzle pieces
Pencil and paper

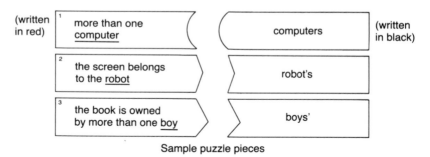

Sample puzzle pieces

Directions to the Learner

[Write on a card kept in the bag]

1 Sort the puzzle pieces into two piles according to color.

2 Put the black pieces back in the bag.

3 Arrange the red pieces in a row according to the numbers in the upper left corner.

4 On your own paper, write the correct plural or possessive form of the underlined nouns, as described by the phrases written in red.

5 When you have written an answer for each piece, remove the puzzle pieces with black writing from the bag. Fit them to the pieces with red writing. Your written answers should match the form given on the corresponding puzzle piece with black writing.

6 When you can get at least 18 out of 20 items correct, show a peer tutor and check the skill off on your progress chart. It feels great to check off those skills!

Strips in a Folder: Manuscript Alphabet

Pinpoint

Think of the alphabet—write manuscript lowercase letters in sequence

Aim

To write lowercase manuscript letters in alphabetical sequence in 30 seconds or less

Feedback Device

The alphabet is written on the inside surface of the back of the folder so the letters appear in the openings under the boxes provided. A piece of construction paper is placed in the folder to cover the answers. When the student finishes writing, he removes the construction paper and compares the letters.

Materials

Laminated manila folder with strips cut out across the front and 26 boxes drawn above the strips; on the inside surface of the back of the folder the lowercase manuscript alphabet is written so the letters appear in the strips under the boxes

Piece of construction paper

Grease pencil or washable acetate marker

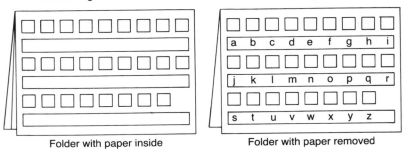

Folder with paper inside   Folder with paper removed

Directions to the Learner

[Write on the back of the folder]

1 Put the colored paper inside the folder.
2 Using the acetate marker, print the alphabet using lowercase letters. Write one letter in each box.
3 When you have finished, take the colored paper out of the folder. Your letters should match the ones you see below them.
4 Practice until you can write the whole alphabet without any mistakes in 30 seconds or less. Do your best!

Suggestions to the Teacher

You can modify this material for uppercase and cursive letters and for numerals. Either sequence or form may be emphasized.

Stylus: Verb Tense Agreement

Pinpoint

See sentence with verb missing—select correct verb tense

Aim

To select the correct verb tense to complete sentences with 90% accuracy on a mastery test

Feedback Device

The student places a stylus in a hole under one of three possible choices to indicate his response. If the response choice is correct, the card can be easily pulled from the pocket with the stylus still in place.

Materials

  Manila file folder cut and taped as illustrated to form a pocket; three holes are cut in the folder under the pocket opening
  4″ x 6″ index cards showing a sentence with the verb missing written at the top of the card and three answer choices written above punched out holes at the bottom of the card
  Stylus

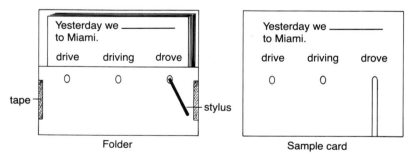

Folder   Sample card

Directions to the Learner

[Write on an index card kept in the pocket]

1. Read the sentence at the top of the card.
2. Decide which of the three verbs completes the sentence correctly. Pay attention to past, present, and future tenses.
3. Put the stylus in the hole under your verb choice.
4. Try to pull the card out of the pocket. If it comes out easily, your answer is correct. If the card does not come out easily, try another form of the verb.
5. When you can complete all the sentences correctly, try the mastery test. It has the same sentences on it, so if you practice, you should get 100%. You can do it!

Windows: Commas

Pinpoint

See dates and addresses without commas—position comma correctly

Aim

To position the comma correctly in 100% of the dates and addresses presented on a set of cards

Feedback Device

When a tab displaying a comma is positioned to indicate the correct placement of the comma, a window on the back of the material reveals an arrow that lines up with an arrow on the back of the tab.

Materials

Piece of tagboard (approximately 8″ x 8″) with a piece of cardboard attached to form a pocket and a window cut out of the tagboard below the pocket; on the back of the tagboard, a window is cut out behind the pocket
Strip of tagboard which slides between two rubber bands on the back of the tagboard (knotted in the front) so the comma on the front of the tab shows in the window; an arrow is drawn on the back of the tab

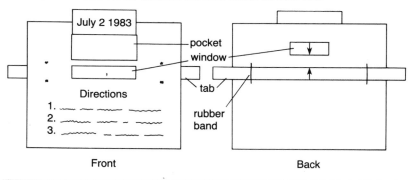

3″ x 5″ index cards showing dates and addresses without commas; an arrow is drawn on the back of each card so that it will line up with the arrow on the back of the tab when the comma on the tab is positioned correctly

Directions to the Learner

[Write on the front of the material]
1 Put one card in the pocket.
2 Slide the tab until the comma is below where it should appear in the date or address.
3 To check your answer, turn the board over. If the arrow on the tab and the arrow in the window line up, your answer is correct. When you can answer all the cards right, you are ready for the Punctuation Mastery Test. Good luck!

Handwriting Scope and Sequence Skills List*

Many handwriting skills are emphasized at more than one grade level. A bullet (•) denotes a skill which has not been emphasized at a previous grade level.

Kindergarten

- Begins to establish a preference for either left- or right-handedness
- Voluntarily draws, paints, and scribbles
- Develops small muscle control through the use of such materials as finger painting, clay, weaving, and puzzles
- Uses tools of writing in making letters, writing names, or attempting to write words
- Understands and applies writing readiness vocabulary given orally, such as left/right, top/bottom, beginning/end, large/small, circle, space, around, across, curve, top line, dotted line, and bottom line
- Begins to establish correct writing position of body, arms, hand, paper, and pencil
- Draws familiar objects using the basic strokes of manuscript writing
- Recognizes and legibly writes own name in manuscript letters using uppercase and lowercase letters appropriately
- Uses writing paper that is standard for manuscript writing

Grade 1

Establishes a preference for either left- or right-handedness

---

*Source: From *Teaching Students with Learning Problems* by C. D. Mercer and A. R. Mercer. Columbus, Ohio: Charles E. Merrill, 1981, pp. 421–24. Reprinted by permission.

Understands and applies writing readiness vocabulary given orally, such as left/right, top/bottom, beginning/end, large/small, circle, space, around, across, curve, top line, dotted line, and bottom line

Draws familiar objects using the basic strokes of manuscript writing

- Begins manuscript writing using both lowercase and uppercase letters introduced to correlate with the child's reading program
- Writes at his desk with correct posture, pencil grip, and paper position, works from left to right, and forms letters in the correct direction

Uses writing paper that is standard for manuscript writing

- Copies words neatly from near position
- Writes with firm strokes and demonstrates good spacing between letters, words, and sentences
- Writes manuscript letters independently and with good firm strokes
- Writes clear, legible manuscript letters at a rate commensurate with ability
- Arranges work neatly and pleasingly on a page (for example, uses margins and paragraph indentions and makes clean erasures)

Grade 2

Establishes a preference for either left- or right-handedness

Uses correct writing position of body, arm, hand, paper, and pencil

Writes with firm strokes and demonstrates good spacing between letters, words, and sentences

Writes clear, legible manuscript letters at a rate commensurate with ability

Arranges work neatly and pleasingly on a page (for example, uses margins and paragraph indentions and makes clean erasures)

- Evaluates writing using a plastic overlay and identifies strengths and weaknesses
- Writes all letters of the alphabet in manuscript from memory

- Recognizes the differences in using manuscript and cursive writing
- Reads simple sentences written in cursive writing on the chalkboard
- Demonstrates physical coordination to proceed to simple cursive writing

Grade 3

Uses correct writing position of body, arm, hand, paper, and pencil

Uses writing paper that is standard for manuscript writing

Evaluates writing using a plastic overlay and identifies strengths and weaknesses

Writes with firm strokes and demonstrates good spacing between letters, words, and sentences

Arranges work neatly and pleasingly on a page (for example, uses margins and paragraph indentions and makes clean erasures)

- Demonstrates ability to decode cursive writing by reading paragraphs of cursive writing both from the chalkboard and from paper
- Identifies cursive lowercase and uppercase letters by matching cursive letters to manuscript letters
- Begins cursive writing with lowercase letters and progresses to uppercase letters as needed
- Uses writing paper that is standard for cursive writing
- Writes all letters of the cursive alphabet using proper techniques in making each letter
- Recognizes the proper joining of letters to form words
- Writes from memory all letters of the alphabet in cursive form

Grade 4

Uses correct writing position of body, arm, hand, paper, and pencil

Evaluates writing using a plastic overlay and identifies strengths and weaknesses

Writes with firm strokes and demonstrates good spacing between letters, words, and sentences

Arranges work neatly and pleasingly on a page (for example, uses margins and paragraph indentions and makes clean erasures)

Uses writing paper that is standard for cursive writing

- Slants and joins the letters in a word and controls spacing between letters
- Uses cursive writing for day-to-day use
- Begins to write with a pen *if* pencil writing is smooth, fluent, and neat
- Maintains and uses manuscript writing for special needs, such as preparing charts, maps, and labels
- Writes clear, legible cursive letters at a rate commensurate with ability

Grade 5

Uses correct writing position of body, arm, hand, paper, and pencil

Evaluates writing using a plastic overlay and identifies strengths and weaknesses

Writes with firm strokes and demonstrates good spacing between letters, words, and sentences

Arranges work neatly and pleasingly on a page (for example, uses margins and paragraph indentions and makes clean erasures)

Uses cursive writing for day-to-day use

Begins to write with a pen *if* pencil writing is smooth, fluent, and neat

Writes clear, legible cursive letters at a rate commensurate with ability

Maintains and uses manuscript writing for special needs, such as preparing charts, maps, and labels

- Reduces size of writing to "adult" proportions of letters (for example, one-quarter space for minimum letters, one-half space for intermediate letters, and three-quarters space for tall lowercase and uppercase letters)
- Takes pride in presenting neat work

Grade 6

Uses correct writing position of body, arm, hand, paper, and pencil

Evaluates writing using a plastic overlay and identifies strengths and weaknesses

Writes with firm strokes and demonstrates good spacing between letters, words, and sentences

Arranges work neatly and pleasingly on a page (for example, uses margins and paragraph indentions and makes clean erasures)

Uses cursive writing for day-to-day use

Begins to write with a pen *if* pencil writing is smooth, fluent, and neat

Maintains and uses manuscript writing for special needs, such as preparing charts, maps, and labels

Reduces size of writing to "adult" proportions of letters (for example, one-quarter space for minimum letters, one-half space for intermediate letters, and three-quarters space for tall lowercase and uppercase letters)

Writes clear, legible cursive letters at a rate commensurate with ability

- Customarily presents neat work
- Evaluates his own progress in the basic handwriting skills pertaining to size, slant, shape, spacing, and alignment

Written Expression Scope and Sequence Skills List*

Kindergarten

Dictates experience stories
Creates pictures for stories he dictates

Grade 1

Capitalization and Punctuation
Copies sentences correctly
Capitalizes first word of a sentence
Capitalizes first letter of a proper name
Uses period at the end of a sentence
Uses question mark after a written question
Uses period after numbers in a list

Written Composition
Arranges scrambled words in correct sentence order
Writes answers to simple questions
Dictates thoughts to scribe and does copy work
Suggests titles for dictated stories
Forms sentences in dictating and in writing
Writes own name and address without using a model
Writes from both personal experience and imagination
Writes given sentences from dictation
Writes phrases that describe location

Creative Expression
Dictates and begins to write captions and comments
about pictures
Writes group poems
Writes riddles, songs, or poems
Creates make-believe stories
Shows increasing selectivity in choice of words to convey
meanings effectively

*Source: From *Teaching Students with Learning Problems* by C. D. Mercer and A. R. Mercer. Columbus, Ohio: Charles E. Merrill, 1981, pp. 425–29. Reprinted by permission.

Grade 2

Capitalization and Punctuation

    Capitalizes titles of compositions

    Capitalizes proper names used in written compositions

    Uses comma after salutation and after closing of a friendly letter

    Uses comma between day of the month and the year

    Uses comma between name of city and state

Written Composition

    Recognizes kinds of sentences—statement and question

    Writes a paragraph of three to five sentences in accordance with prespecified criteria: relate to topic, capitalize first word of each sentence, use correct end punctuation, indent first line

    Supplies titles for sentence groups

    Writes given sentences from dictation

    Copies sentences correctly

Creative Expression

    Responds to sensory stimuli with descriptive words

    Uses a variety of descriptive words or phrases

    Writes imaginative stories in which ideas and feelings are expressed

    Draws pictures to express a theme, to inform, or to persuade

Grade 3

Capitalization and Punctuation

    Capitalizes correctly the names of months, days, holidays; first word in a line of verse; titles of books, stories, poems; salutation and closing of letters and notes; and names of special places

    Begins to apply correct punctuation for abbreviations, initials, contractions, items in a list, quotations, questions, and exclamations

    Uses proper indention for paragraphs

Written Composition

    Gives written explanations using careful selection, relevant details, and sequential order

    Begins to proofread for accuracy and to do occasional revising

Writes simple thank-you notes using correct form
Builds ideas into paragraphs
Uses a variety of sentences
Combines short, choppy sentences into longer ones
Avoids run-on sentences
Keeps to one idea
Correctly sequences ideas in sentences
Finds and deletes sentences that do not belong in a paragraph

Creative Expression

Writes imaginative stories—imagines how others feel or how he might feel in another situation
Uses a variety of words to express action, mood, sound, and feeling
Writes original poetry
Writes interesting dialogue

Grade 4

Capitalization and Punctuation

Uses capital letters correctly in the following areas: proper nouns, first word of poetry line, principal words in titles, common and proper nouns, seasons as common nouns
Uses commas correctly in the following areas: after introductory adverbial clause, to set off interjections, to separate items in a series, to separate coordinate clauses, to set off words in direct address, after salutation
Uses periods correctly after declarative sentences
Uses apostrophes correctly to show possession

Written Composition

Makes simple outline with main ideas
Proofreads for accuracy in writing
Uses correct form and mechanics in writing invitations and business letters
Compiles a list of books read, including the title and author of the books and their subjects
Writes a paragraph defining a term, using an example

Creative Expression

Writes descriptions of people, places, events
Writes narrative paragraphs in which events are presented chronologically

Writes a story including characters, setting, and plot

Distinguishes between imaginative and factual description

Writes a brief story in response to a picture

Grade 5

Capitalization and Punctuation

Uses uppercase correctly in the following areas: first word of poetry line, first word of direct quotation, seasons as common nouns, ordinary position titles (not capitalized)

Uses commas correctly in the following areas: after introductory phrases, to set off nonrestrictive clauses, in addresses, in dates, to separate subordinate clause from main clause, to set off appositive, to set off parenthetical elements, to separate quotations from rest of sentence

Uses periods correctly

Uses colons after introductory lines

Uses apostrophes correctly in contractions and to show possession, and not in possessive pronouns

Uses quotation marks correctly in direct quotations

Uses hyphens in compound numbers

Uses semicolons correctly with coordinate clauses

Written Composition

Uses a variety of sentences—declarative, interrogative, exclamatory, and imperative

Uses compound subjects and compound predicates

Writes paragraph from outline

Begins to organize writing by adhering to one subject and striving for a continuous thought flow

Produces a factual report from notes and an outline

Outlines main ideas (I, II, III) and subordinate ideas (A, B, C)

Edits writing for errors in spelling, capitalization, punctuation, and usage

Writes a paragraph which contains a topic sentence based upon a fact and supports that fact with at least three additional facts

Creative Expression

> Records and expands sensory images, observations, memories, opinions, and individual impressions
>
> Writes patterned and free verse
>
> Develops a story plot including at least two characters, a challenge or a struggle, and a climax which results from events that prepare the reader
>
> Writes short scripts based on stories read by the group

Grade 6

Capitalization and Punctuation

> Capitalizes names of outline divisions
>
> Writes correctly punctuated dialogue
>
> Correctly punctuates dictated paragraphs
>
> Uses underlining and quotation marks correctly for titles
>
> Edits own writing for correct spelling, punctuation, capitalization, and usage

Written Composition

> Develops concise statements by avoiding wordiness
>
> Uses complex sentences
>
> Checks paragraph for accurate statements
>
> Uses transition words to connect ideas
>
> Shows improvement in complete composition—introduction, development, and conclusion
>
> Writes from point of view that is consistent with the intention
>
> Plans carefully before beginning to write and revises periodically
>
> Edits all writing to be read by another person and revises it in accordance with accepted mechanics of writing
>
> Writes a well-constructed paragraph (topic sentence, supporting details, and conclusion)
>
> Writes a newspaper story from given facts
>
> Narrows topics for reports
>
> Writes a paragraph of comparison and contrast
>
> Uses correct form for business letters

Creative Expression

> Uses figurative language—similes, metaphors
>
> Writes descriptions and narratives
>
> Writes a variety of prose and verse based on personal experience

Writes a variety of short fiction—tall tales, fables, mysteries, adventure stories

Describes a character by including details (the way the character looks, behaves, dresses, or speaks)

Writes original scripts to be produced by groups in the class

8

MATERIALS FOR OTHER SUBJECTS

This chapter features the use of self-correcting materials for a variety of subjects (for example, biology, Spanish, social studies, home economics, etc.). These materials enable the teacher to individualize seatwork, homework, or peer teaching activities. Their usefulness in teaching specific subject content can be extensive—provided that learner needs (skill areas) are identified and translated into practice activities in one of the numerous self-correcting formats.

Answer on Back: Biology

Pinpoint

See definition—say term

Aim

To say with 90% accuracy the correct scientific term after reading its definition

Feedback Device

The corresponding term is written in blue on the reverse side of the card containing its definition.

Materials

Index cards with a definition written in black on one side and the appropriate scientific term written in blue on the reverse side

Directions to the Learner

[Write on the top card in the deck]
1. Sort the cards so the black printing is facing you.
2. Read the definition.

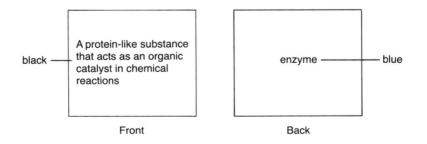

3 Say to yourself the term the definition describes.

4 Check your answer by looking on the reverse side of the card. When you can correctly identify 90% of the definitions (23 out of 25), you may begin work on the next unit.

Cassette: Spanish

Pinpoint

Hear paragraph in Spanish—write English translation

Aim

To translate a paragraph from oral Spanish to written English with two or fewer errors in meaning, tense, and structure after practicing with the self-correcting cassette tape

Feedback Device

The student hears the English translation on the cassette tape following the presentation of the paragraph in Spanish.

Materials

Cassette tape recorder
Cassette tape prepared with a paragraph presented in
    Spanish; the English translation follows the Spanish
    presentation
Spanish/English dictionary
Pencil and paper

Directions to the Learner

[Record on the tape]
1   Listen to the following paragraph presented in Spanish. The paragraph will be part of your next exam in class.
2   Write an English translation. You may stop the tape and replay it as many times as necessary.
3   When you have finished writing your translation, continue playing the tape to listen to the English translation. Check your work. You do not have to match the tape exactly, but you should have the same meaning, tense, and

structure for your sentences. It is all right to use synonyms. If you are unsure whether you have translated a Spanish word into an acceptable English synonym, use the Spanish/English dictionary.

4 Practice with the tape as many times as you wish before the exam.

Colored Acetate Folder: Home Economics

Pinpoint

See recipe measurements—write doubled quantities

Aim

To be able to double the measurements of a recipe and write the quantities with 100% accuracy before preparing the food

Feedback Device

The original recipe is written in black and the doubled quantity for each ingredient is written in yellow. When the sheet is placed in a colored acetate folder, the yellow writing cannot be seen. The learner writes the doubled measurements on the acetate with a marker and then checks his answers with the measures written in yellow by removing the sheet from the folder.

Materials

Colored acetate folder (red is best)
Grease pencil or washable acetate marker
Worksheet with a recipe written in black and the doubled quantity for each ingredient written with a yellow felt-tip marker

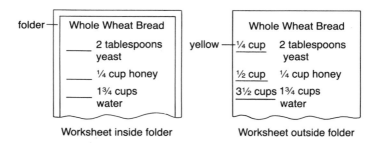

Worksheet inside folder   Worksheet outside folder

Directions to the Learner

[Write on the back of the worksheet]

1 Place this recipe sheet in the colored folder. You will make a double recipe—but first you must write the doubled measures.

2 Use a washable acetate marker or a grease pencil to write the doubled quantities on the acetate folder next to each ingredient. Write the measurement that will require the least effort to measure. For example, 1½ teaspoons doubled is 3 teaspoons, but it is easier to measure 1 tablespoon.

3 When you have doubled the entire recipe, pull the sheet out of the folder. Check the measurements you wrote with the ones written in yellow on the recipe sheet.

4 When you can write correctly all of the doubled measurements, put the recipe sheet back in the folder and line up the doubled quantities with the correct ingredients.

5 Go ahead and prepare the recipe. The results should be great!

Suggestions to the Teacher

The acetate folder will also protect the recipe sheet from being soiled as the recipe is being prepared.

Flap: Geography

Pinpoint

See illustration—say name of geographic feature

Aim

To be able to view illustrations and say the names of 95% of the presented geographic features in a demonstration for a study partner

Feedback Device

The correct answer is hidden by a flap. After making a response, the student raises the flap to check his answer.

Materials

Heavyweight clear plastic sandwich bag which has a vinyl flap attached to it near the bottom

Index cards (slightly smaller than the plastic bag) which show an illustration of a geographic feature and have the name of the feature written near the bottom of the card

Cards inside bag

Sample card

Directions to the Learner

[Write on the top card of the deck]

1 To practice naming the geographic features which have been introduced in class, leave the cards in this bag and look at the top card. The feature to name is indicated by the arrow.

2 Say the name of the feature to yourself.

3 To check your answer, raise the vinyl flap and you will see the name of the feature. If you are right, remove the card from the bag. If your answer did not match the one under the flap, put the card behind the others in the bag for further review.

4 Practice until you can complete all the cards and say the correct name on your first try.

5 Tell your study partner you are ready to demonstrate this skill. You are allowed to miss one card and still record that you have mastered this skill. With all of this practice, you probably will get a perfect score. You can do it!

Holes: Social Studies

Pinpoint

See name of a nation—select capital city

Aim

To select with 100% accuracy the correct capital of the European nations presented in a demonstration for the classroom aide

Feedback Device

Items are presented in a multiple-choice format, with a hole punched below each choice. The student selects an answer by inserting a stylus through the hole under his selection. The student then looks on the back of the card. If the stylus is in the hole circled in a color, his choice is correct.

Materials

Index cards with the name of a European nation at the top and three possible capital city choices written above punched out holes at the bottom; on the back, the hole indicating the correct answer is circled in a color
Stylus, pencil, or thin stick

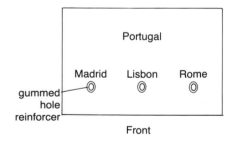
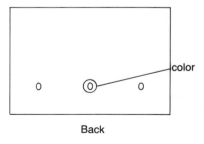

Front   Back

Directions to the Learner

[Write on the top card of the deck]

1 Read the name of the European nation at the top of the card. Below the name of the country are the names of three cities. One city is the nation's capital.

2 Select the nation's capital by inserting the stylus in the hole under your choice.

3 Check your answer by looking on the back of the card. If the stylus is in the hole circled in a color, you have made the correct choice.

4 When you can complete all the cards correctly on the first try, show your skill to the classroom aide.

Light: Consumer Education

Pinpoint

See price and volume of two brands of the same product—select the more economical of the two brands

Aim

To calculate the unit price of two different brands of the same product when given the price and volume, and then to select the better buy of the two brands with 100% accuracy

Feedback Device

When the correct answer hole is selected with the stylus, an electrical circuit is completed and a small light bulb is illuminated.

Materials

Electric Learning Board (see chapter 2 for a list of materials and construction guidelines)
5" x 8" stimulus cards with the name of a product and two choices of price and volume
Pencil and paper

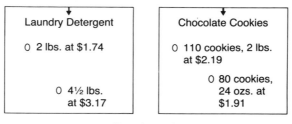

Sample cards

Directions to the Learner

[Write on cover card for the pack]

1   Place one card on the board by lining up the arrow on the card with the arrow on the board.

2   Read the product name and the two choices of volume and price. Sometimes the most economical way to buy products is *not* to buy the one with the smallest price tag. Good shoppers look at the price per unit to find the best buy.

3   To calculate the unit prices on your paper, first be sure the products are measured in the same units so they can be compared. Make any necessary conversions. Then divide the price by the number of units. For example: 12 oz. at 60¢; .60 ÷ 12 = .05; the unit price is 5¢ per ounce.

4   Compare the unit prices for the two products and decide which is cheaper.

5   Place the stylus into the hole next to your choice for the better buy. If you are right, the light will come on. Good job! You are a smart consumer.

6   Practice until you can select the better buy on your first attempt on each product.

Matching: Earth Science

Pinpoint

See picture and name of rocks—say classification (sedimentary, igneous, or metamorphic)

Aim

To say with 90% accuracy the classifications of different rocks as sedimentary, igneous, or metamorphic, after looking at cards containing a picture and name of the rock, during an individual exam with the lab instructor

Feedback Device

When the clip is positioned next to the name of the correct category on the front of the material, the symbol on the back of the stimulus card matches the symbol inside the clip on the back of the material.

Materials

8" x 12" piece of tagboard with a 5" x 5" piece of clear plastic attached to it to form a pocket; the piece of tagboard is creased so it can be folded and the words *sedimentary, igneous,* and *metamorphic* are written to the right of the crease and a symbol for each classification is drawn on the back

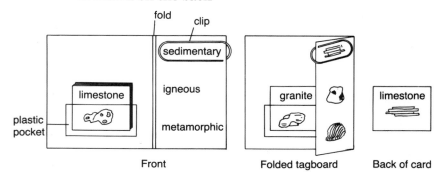

4″ x 6″ index cards showing an illustration and the name of a rock; on the back, the name of the rock is written and the appropriate symbol for its classification is drawn

Large plastic paper clip

Directions to the Learner

[Write on the top card of the deck]

1   Look at each index card in this pocket which shows a name and picture of different rocks. Your task is to classify each rock as sedimentary, igneous, or metamorphic.

2   Say the classification for each rock to yourself and position the clip on the tagboard so it points to the category.

3   To check your answer, take the card out of the pocket. Fold over the right edge of the material and see if the symbol inside the clip matches the one on the back of the card. If they match, you chose the right category. If the symbols do not match, find what the right answer is, and put the card behind the other cards in the pocket to try again.

4   When you can complete the entire set of 50 cards with five or fewer errors, sign up for an individual exam appointment with your lab instructor. You will have to look at the same set of cards and say the classification with 90% accuracy. After practicing, you should pass with flying colors!

Pockets: United States Government

Pinpoint

See phrase describing government function—classify the function as legislative, judicial, or executive

Aim

To classify with 100% accuracy various government functions according to the branch responsible, in a demonstration for the teacher

Feedback Device

When the functions written on strips of tagboard have been sorted into the proper pockets, the reverse sides of each set of strips may be arranged to form three complete illustrations.

Materials

Three pieces of 8" x 8" tagboard (one for each government branch), cut into strips after a government function is written on each strip on the front and a large illustration is glued to the back of each piece of tagboard
Three business-size envelopes, labeled legislative, judicial, and executive
9" x 12" envelope for storing the material

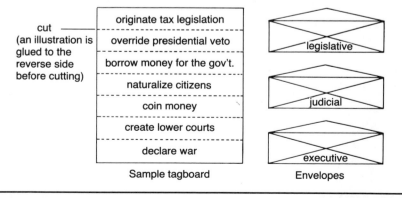

cut
(an illustration is glued to the reverse side before cutting)

originate tax legislation
override presidential veto
borrow money for the gov't.
naturalize citizens
coin money
create lower courts
declare war

Sample tagboard

legislative

judicial

executive

Envelopes

Directions to the Learner

[Write on the outside of the 9″ x 12″ envelope]

1 Remove the three letter-size envelopes and the strips of tagboard from this envelope.

2 Sort the strips so that the sides with words written on them are showing. Each strip describes a function of the federal government. You must decide which branch (legislative, judicial, or executive) is responsible for that function.

3 Sort the strips into the three envelopes according to the branch of government labeled on the envelope.

4 Check your answers by looking at the back sides of the strips from an envelope and arranging them to form a complete picture. If you classified the functions correctly, you will have three complete pictures, one from each envelope. If some of the strips are not in the right envelope, find their correct group. Then mix the strips up and try again.

5 When you feel confident that you can classify each function correctly, sign up on the success chart and the teacher will watch you demonstrate what you have learned.

Puzzles: Chemistry

Pinpoint

See name of element—write chemical notation

Aim

To write the chemical notation for various elements with 100% accuracy on a written exam

Feedback Device

After looking at the puzzle pieces with the names of the elements and writing a response, the student fits the two-piece puzzles together to reveal the matching chemical notations.

Materials

Commercial puzzle (does not have to be a complete puzzle) with chemical elements' names written in blue and the corresponding chemical notations written in brown on the backs of connecting puzzle pieces
Small box to hold puzzle pieces
Pencil and paper

Directions to the Learner

[Write on the top of the box]
    1 Sort the puzzle pieces into two piles according to the color of the writing on the puzzle piece.

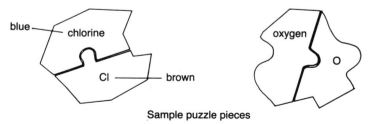

Sample puzzle pieces

2   Look at the pieces with the names of the elements written in blue.

3   Write the chemical notation for each element on your paper, and arrange these pieces in a row on your desk in the order that you used them.

4   When you have finished writing all the elements' notations, match the puzzle pieces with the pieces with notations written in brown on them. Each pair will form a two-piece puzzle and does not have to fit with any other pieces. Be sure to keep the elements in the order that you recorded your responses on your paper.

5   When you have fitted the puzzle pieces together, check the notations on the puzzle pieces with the ones you wrote on your paper.

6   Practice until you can write the notations with 100% accuracy. When you are ready, you can take the written exam on chemical notations. You will be allowed to start working in the chemistry lab as soon as you pass the exam.

Suggestions to the Teacher

To assure that only one puzzle piece showing a chemical notation will match with an element's name, first assemble the puzzle on a large board with the illustration side up. (This can be a reward activity for students.) Then turn the puzzle over to the blank side. Label the puzzle pieces while the puzzle is assembled, and avoid labeling more than one connecting piece for an element's name with a chemical notation. Each two-piece puzzle should have only one possible match with contrasting color labels.

Strips in a Folder: Physical Education

Pinpoint

See tennis question—write correct tennis rule

Aim

To answer the questions correctly on a written exam covering the rules of tennis, as a prerequisite to acting as a judge during intramural tennis matches

Feedback Device

The strips cut in a folder cover the answers but reveal the questions. After writing his responses, the student pulls the worksheet upward to show the answers in the spaces where the questions previously appeared.

Materials

Laminated manila folder with strips cut out of the front
Washable acetate marker or grease pencil
Damp cloth
Worksheets containing tennis questions with the answers written below each question

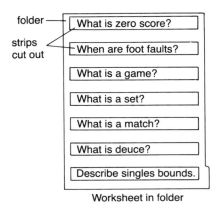

folder
strips cut out

What is zero score?
When are foot faults?
What is a game?
What is a set?
What is a match?
What is deuce?
Describe singles bounds.

Worksheet in folder

What is zero score?
  Love
When are foot faults?
  During service
What is a game?
  Point after 40
What is a set?
  6 games, up by 2
What is a match?
  Best 2 of 3 sets
What is deuce?
  Tie at 40
Describe singles bounds.
  Inside long lines

Sample worksheet

Directions to the Learner

[Write on the back of the folder]

1. Read the questions on the worksheets in the folder. These are the same questions that will appear on your written judges' exam. You must score 100% before you will be allowed to work at intramural matches.

2. To practice the questions, write your answer to each question with a washable marker on the strip below each question.

3. To check your answers after you have completed a worksheet, pull the worksheet upward to reveal the answers in the strip openings.

4. Correct any mistakes and then wipe the strips clean with a damp cloth.

5. Remove the first worksheet and align the second one so only the questions are showing.

6. Repeat the entire procedure for all the worksheets. By practicing with these worksheets, you should be able to take the exam sooner than you think. You'll be out on the courts in no time! Good job!

Stylus: Literature

Pinpoint

See title—select author

Aim

To select the correct author for 100% of the given titles in Twentieth Century American fiction, in a demonstration for a peer tutor

Feedback Device

When the stylus is inserted in the hole under the correct answer, the card can be easily pulled from the pocket.

Materials

Piece of 6″ x 8″ heavy felt, folded and sewn to form a pocket; three holes are evenly spaced across the front of the pocket

5″ x 8″ index cards with a title on the top of the card and three author answer choices above punched out holes at the bottom of the card

Stylus, pencil, or thin stick

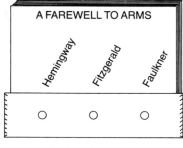

Cards in felt pocket

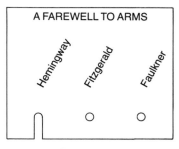

Sample card

Directions to the Learner

[Write on the top card of the deck]

1   On each card read the title of a piece of Twentieth Century American fiction and below that the names of three authors.

2   Select the author of the piece by putting the stylus in the hole under your answer choice.

3   Check your answer by pulling gently on the card with the stylus in place. If the card pulls out easily, you selected the right answer. If the card resists, try another choice. Put all cards that needed a second or third try back in the pocket behind the other cards.

4   Keep practicing until you can complete all the cards on the first try. Then sign up with a peer tutor for a demonstration. If you are 100% successful, get your tutor's signature next to this skill on your hierarchy.

Windows: History

Pinpoint

See description of American historical event—say the century in which the event occurred

Aim

To identify the century in which an American historical event occurred, with 80% accuracy on 40 events during a demonstration for the classroom aide

Feedback Device

A set of cards is contained in a pocket with a window cut in the back. The cards have dates on the back and are sequenced so that the answer to the card appearing on top is revealed in the back window.

Materials

5" x 8" piece of tagboard, folded and taped to form a 5" x 4" pocket; a window is cut in the back of the pocket
4" x 6" index cards, numbered 1 to 40 in the upper left corner, with a description of an American historical event written on the front and a date (according to the card sequence) written on the back so it will show in the window

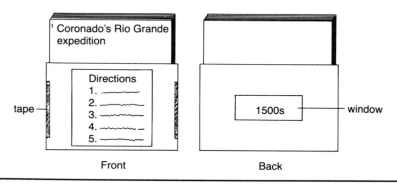

Front   Back

Directions to the Learner

[Write on the front of the pocket]

1 Check to be sure that all the cards in this pocket are in sequence from 1 to 40.

2 Read the description of the event in American history and say to yourself the century in which it occurred.

3 Turn the pocket over and look in the window to check your answer.

4 Put the top card in the back of the deck in the pocket and respond to the event on the next card.

5 When you can answer the set of 40 cards with three or fewer errors, tell the aide that you are ready for a demonstration. If you can say the right century for 37 or more events, you can cross this skill off your progress chart. Good job!

9

COMMERCIAL MATERIALS

Numerous commercial materials utilize a self-correcting format and present skills in various content areas. Although many available materials include an answer key, the selected materials described in this section offer a unique method of self-correction. These materials provide the teacher with ready-made self-correction devices and also offer formats that may be adaptable to teacher-made materials. The addresses of the publishers and producers of the materials are listed at the end of the chapter.

Action Mark, Paper Response System

Publisher: 3M Company
Description: Instructional answer sheets and teaching sheets are printed with visible and invisible print. The invisible print can be revealed by coloring the answer box with an Action Mark

crayon. A series of math worksheets is available that provides drill on addition, subtraction, multiplication, division, metric measurement, and reading a clock and a calendar. The instructional answer sheets are available in multiple choice and true/false formats. These sheets can be adapted for any teacher-made or commercial test. The Action Mark crayons are nontoxic.

Alphabet Zoo Activities

Publisher: Developmental Learning Materials
Description: The material contains 26 two-piece puzzles that involve matching an alphabet letter with an illustration of a zoo animal. The two-piece puzzles interlock only if the match is correct and thus are self-correcting. A brief description of each animal is given on the poster tray.

Coin Puzzles

Publisher: Developmental Learning Materials
Description: These two-piece puzzles require unique matches for completion and provide feedback to the learner about the correctness of a response. The top part of each puzzle shows an array of coins, and the bottom part shows their monetary value.

Diagger Math Tutors

Publisher: Educational Teaching Aids
Description: A series of Math Tutor sets is available for instruction in place value, grouping, basic operations, money, and "smaller than." The sets include work cards, a work tray, and answer chips. The answer chips form a puzzle that will fit together only when correct answers are selected.

Duorama

Publisher: Educational Teaching Aids
Description: Duorama games are available in 13 sets, each including 10 games. Most games have eight questions and eight answers. The student places answer tiles in a clear plastic case. The case is closed and turned over to reveal a picture formed by correct responses.

Flip and Learn: Money

Publisher: Developmental Learning Materials
Description: Students gain practice in identifying, counting, and totaling coins. Answers on the back of each card provide immediate feedback and make the material self-correcting.

Flip and Learn: Time

Publisher: Developmental Learning Materials
Description: Students practice reading time from illustrations of clock faces and check their answers by turning the cards over to read the correct answers on the backs of the cards. Cards present different styles of clocks and different levels of difficulty.

Green Mountain Math—Fractions and Decimals

Publisher: Dormac
Description: The two math series are designed for use by hearing impaired, learning disabled, and high school or postsecondary students. The workbooks include highly visual techniques for explaining computations and procedures in a semiprogrammed format. The solutions are illustrated in the left margin of each page and may be covered during practice and uncovered for feedback.

Homonym Tales

Publisher: Curriculum Associates
Description: This series of spirit masters is appropriate for grades four through eight and teaches the usage of several hundred homonyms in a series of 30 interesting short stories. Proper meaning and spelling of the homonyms are emphasized. Thirty answer cards for student use make the material self-correcting.

Independent Drill for Mastery: Fundamentals of Addition and Subtraction, Fundamentals of Multiplication and Division

Publisher: Developmental Learning Materials
Description: The material is designed to increase students' speed and accuracy in computation, especially in basic math facts. Students self-correct practice papers before the teacher administers a study-test. Each program (addition/subtraction and multiplication/division) includes a teacher's manual, award certificates, scoring overlays, spirit masters, progress records, and class profiles.

Independent Drill for Mastery: Fundamentals of Spelling

Publisher: Developmental Learning Materials
Description: This spelling program is self-correcting during the practice phase. Students listen to self-study lessons on tape and then correct their own practice papers with answer/study sheets. Students decide when they are prepared for the mastery test, which is administered by the teacher.

Money Wheel

Publisher: Developmental Learning Materials
Description: The material requires the learner to match a picture, a numeral, and a word representation of money amounts from 1¢ to $5. Discs move until they all represent the same amount of money, and answers are on the back.

Moving Up in Grammar—Capitalization and Punctuation

Publisher: Developmental Learning Materials
Description: The kit is designed to improve the capitalization and punctuation skills of 4th through 6th grade students. Answer cards kept with the kit make the material self-correcting. The kit also includes a class profile sheet for record keeping and award certificates to reinforce student progress.

Necessary Arithmetic Skills

Publisher: Gamco Industries
Description: Five different filmstrip series covering basic arithmetic skills, measurement, fractions, decimal fractions, and percent include filmstrips and cassettes. Students view and hear a sample problem and its solution, respond to a similar problem, and, finally, are given an explanation of the solution. This material features a multisensory approach.

Noun Puzzles and Verb Puzzles

Publisher: Developmental Learning Materials
Description: The top section of each puzzle illustrates an object or an action, and the bottom section provides its printed name. The sections interlock only if they belong together. Each set of puzzles includes 48 words.

Opposites

Publisher: Educational Teaching Aids
Description: The set of 26 two-piece puzzles matches antonyms or opposites to teach vocabulary to beginning readers. Each word card has a unique cut that will only match with a word having the opposite meaning. Similar sets of puzzles are available from ETA for instruction in sequencing, survival signs, color names, and number concepts.

Outline-Building

Publisher: Curriculum Associates
Description: The material contains 24 outline sets that require the student to arrange a series of small cards into main topics, subtopics, and details for an outline. This manipulative activity provides a concrete approach to the task of outlining. Students may check their work by using the separate answer cards provided. The content is aimed at students in grades five through nine.

Paragraphing Kit

Publisher: Curriculum Associates
Description: This kit contains 120 lesson cards designed to help students analyze and demonstrate the skill of writing paragraphs. Students in grades five through nine may use the materials for small-group or individual instruction and practice. Answers are accessible to the learner on tab cards kept with the kit.

Peek-A-Boo

Publisher: Reading Joy
Description: The Peek-A-Boo materials provide immediate feedback to the learner after a response is made. Clear vinyl pockets hold answer sticks that are flipped over to check the accuracy of a response. A variety of Peek-A-Boo sets is available in readiness, reading, and bilingual academic areas.

Prefix Puzzles and Suffix Puzzles

Publisher: Developmental Learning Materials
Description: These two-piece puzzles include a base word and an affix. The prefixes and suffixes may each be matched to three different base words. A sentence using each completed puzzle word is printed on each puzzle back.

Quizkid Speller

Publisher: Gamco Industries
Description: The electronic, calculator-type device has three modes of operation: Learn, Spell, and Game. The game book illustrates words on six different levels of difficulty. In the Learn and Spell modes, the display shows 10 randomly selected page numbers from the game book. The student presses alphabet keys to spell a word and receives a green light if his spelling is correct and a red light if his spelling is incorrect. The device calculates a score for each series: five points for a correct first try, three points for a correct second try, and one point for a correct third try. In the Game mode, two or more players may play.

Shape-Ups

Publisher: Reading Joy
Description: The self-correcting puzzles reinforce correct responses and are available for 18 different phonic, vocabulary, and reading skills. Two open-ended plastic laminated puzzles are available for the teacher who wants to create individualized self-correcting materials.

Sound and Symbol Puzzles

Publisher: Developmental Learning Materials
Description: The self-correcting puzzles require students to match a letter of the alphabet with an object that begins with that letter. Uniquely shaped puzzle pieces require correct matches for completion of the puzzle.

Spelling B

Producer: Texas Instruments
Description: This electronic learning aid presents over 260 words at three levels of difficulty. A picture book accompanies the calculator-like aid. The machine displays a number and the student then locates the numbered picture in the book and spells the word by pressing letter keys. The machine signals "right" or "wrong" and gives the correct spelling after two wrong attempts. A score is displayed after each set of five words. Several spelling games are also included.

Stretchy Spaghetti

Publisher: Reading Joy
Description: Students respond to questions by stretching colored strands of "spaghetti" to connect with an answer. A color code on the back of the material matches with the colored strand to indicate a correct response. Kits available include open-ended, readiness, word attack, and comprehension activities.

Telor Learning System

Publisher: Mafex Associates
Description: The hand-held device features interchangeable teaching lessons in cartridge format. The cartridges contain up to 40 frames and cover math, measurement, geometry, reading, and perceptual skills. The choice of a correct answer advances the lesson to the next frame. No batteries or electricity are involved.

Thirty Lessons in Outlining

Publisher: Curriculum Associates
Description: No teacher direction is required for this series of lessons. The subskills needed for organizing outlines are presented through simple, clear directions and follow a logical sequence. The vocabulary and comprehension level are controlled to a fourth-grade level. Acceptable answers are provided on separate answer sheets, allowing students to correct their own work.

Tutorgram

Publisher: Opportunities for Learning
Description: The Tutorgram system includes an electronic unit and programs made up of 54 plastic probe cards. The student places a probe card on the unit and inserts a probe in a hole corresponding to an answer. If the choice is correct, a light and/or buzzer will activate, providing feedback for the learner. Over 60 different programs covering a variety of academic skills are available.

United States Map Games and World Map Games

Publisher: Developmental Learning Materials
Description: Both games give learners feedback as they take turns locating sites on a map. The player throws a pair of dice and looks at a table to find a site listed by the two numbers on the dice. The player then locates a marker on the map covering the site. The student checks the answer by lifting the marker to

see if the number underneath matches the number from the table.

Versa-Tiles

Publisher: Educational Teaching Aids
Description: Versa-Tiles are available in kits that emphasize vocabulary, spelling, logic, math, reading, or language skills. For all kits, students respond by arranging letter or number tiles in an answer case. The answer case closes and flips the tiles over. Geometric shapes on the back of each tile form patterns that are checked against a key in the bottom portion of the worksheets.

Word Analysis Kit

Publisher: Curriculum Associates
Description: The kit contains a series of cards containing at least 24 words each and several category headings that focus on meaning. The student writes the words under the proper headings and then checks his work with the answers given on the reverse side of the card. The material is designed for students working at first- through third-grade levels.

Word Growth II—Spelling Kit

Publisher: Curriculum Associates
Description: This kit includes spelling activities for high achievers in grades four through eight. Words are presented in list form and in context. A test-study-test method is used, with corrected tests available to the student for immediate feedback. Each student records his own progress and advances at an individual rate. The reusable material provides 120 self-directing lessons.

Addresses of Publishers and Producers

Curriculum Associates
5 Esquire Road
North Billerica, MA 01862

Developmental Learning Materials
P.O. Box 4000
One DLM Park
Allen, TX 75002

Dormac
P.O. Box 752
Beaverton, OR 97075

Educational Teaching Aids
159 West Kinzie Street
Chicago, IL 60610

Gamco Industries
Box 1862B
Big Spring, TX 79720

Mafex Associates
90 Cherry Street
Box 519
Johnstown, PA 15907

Opportunities for Learning
8950 Lurline Avenue
Chatsworth, CA 91311

Reading Joy
P.O. Box 404
Naperville, IL 60540

Texas Instruments
2305 University Avenue
Lubbock, TX 79415

3M Company
Box 33050
Dept. YBS-46
St. Paul, MN 55101

SELF-CORRECTION AND COMPUTER SOFTWARE

Computer technology has arrived in the classroom. Teachers use microcomputers to keep records, tutor students, reward good classroom behavior, and assess academic achievement. Instructional computer programs can provide drill and practice or emphasize problem solving. Some software presents academics in game-playing formats or simulations of real and imaginary events. When a student works independently at the classroom computer, the quality of the instructional software and the teacher's wisdom in matching lesson to student will determine if the time at the computer results in learning.

Computers are ideal for providing students with feedback as they enter responses. The clever programmer can design software that gives students immediate feedback in forms that are meaningful, fun, and personalized. This chapter discusses self-correction as a feature of educational computer software and provides suggestions to the teacher purchasing software for student use. There is a glossary of selected computer terms at the end of the chapter.

Software and Self-Correction

Students working independently at computers have the same needs as students working independently at desks, including the need for feedback. Instructional computer programs can provide feedback and inform the learner as to whether his response is correct or incorrect. However, not all computerized feedback is equally effective. Feedback may appear only as a score at the end of a lesson, or as an entire supplementary lesson based on the type of error. Those responsible for purchasing educational software should be aware of the types of self-correction provided in instructional computer programs.

Reinforcing Correct Answers

Immediacy of feedback. If a learner receives a positive reinforcer for a correct response, it is likely that he will repeat the same response in the future. Instructional software can be designed to deliver positive reinforcers immediately after each correct response. If the learner is young or is working on a new task, it may be especially important to receive feedback after each correct response. Some educational software does not reinforce every correct response, but instead gives the learner a score at the end of the lesson according to the number of correct responses. This type of feedback does not necessarily help the student learn to make correct responses. Unless the learner scores 100% correct, or receives feedback after making errors, the learner does not know which items were correct and which were incorrect.

The speed with which feedback is presented to the learner can be an important factor in a computerized lesson. If the screen has to clear for an illustration or message to appear after each correct response, the pace of the lesson may not hold the student's interest. Animated figures that appear to be cheering or jumping up and down after correct answers may initially seem appealing, but some learners quickly become bored or off-task in the 10 to 20 seconds required by some reinforcement animations. One quick type of feedback is simply the appearance of the next item as soon as the student enters a correct response.

Personalized feedback. Reinforcing feedback can be personalized with the learner's name. Some programs require the student to enter his name at the beginning of the lesson, the purpose of which may be to display the learner's name in a reinforcing sentence or phrase, such as "Good work, Megan!" or "You got that one right, Jeff!" Seeing their names on the computer screen can be very exciting for students. A variety of phrases within the same lesson is more interesting than a consistent, predictable message.

Examples of software that deliver reinforcement. Computer programmers have devised some unique and motivating self-correcting features for educational software. One example is "Problem Areas in Addition, Part 1" from the Society for Visual Education (SVE). The lesson covers addition of large numbers. Reinforcement for a correct answer is a display citing a fact from the Guinness World Records that relates to the sum of the problem. Another SVE program, "Problem Areas in Subtraction, Part 2," rewards correct answers with a series of clues in a mystery story. This software requires that the teacher be aware of the learner's reading level. Some students perform math and reading tasks at different grade levels, and if the learner cannot read the Guinness facts or the mystery clues, the correction will not be very reinforcing.

A gamelike format has been used successfully in many educational materials. Computer software for the classroom now often looks like the popular and attractive video arcade games. Developmental Learning Materials publishes a set of software called "Arcademic Skill Builders" featuring math and language arts skills, with graphics that resemble arcade games. The software allows the student or teacher to select from nine different speeds, and games last from one to five minutes.

Each correct response in the Arcademic programs results in a change in the video screen, and sometimes a running tally of hits and misses is kept at the bottom of the screen. The student does not receive the correct answer when he makes an error; thus, this software works best with students who can use another method to find the correct answer or with those students who may be accurate but slow. This software would be classified as a drill and practice program rather than a tutorial program. Since it is often difficult to motivate students for drill and practice, the Arcademic Skill Builders and similar arcadelike software may be useful in the classroom. (See Table 10.1 for a list of companies that publish some software featuring self-correction.)

Table 10.1 *Publishers of self-correcting software*

Borg-Warner Educational Systems, 600 West University Drive, Arlington Heights, Illinois 60004-9990

Developmental Learning Materials, P.O. Box 4000, Allen, Texas 75002

Dorsett Educational Systems, P.O. Box 1226, Norman, Oklahoma 73070

Educational Activities, P.O. Box 392, Freeport, New York 11520

Educational Computing Systems, 136 Fairbanks Road, Oak Ridge, Tennessee 37830

Educational Software Consultants, P.O. Box 30846, Orlando, Florida 32862

Educational Teaching Aids, 159 West Kinzie Street, Chicago, Illinois 60610

Hart, 8 Baird Mountain Road, Asheville, North Carolina 28804

Hartley Courseware, Box 431, Dimondale, Michigan 48821

Love Publishing Company, 1777 South Bellaire Street, Denver, Colorado 80222

MEDIA Materials, Department 830151, 2936 Remington Avenue, Baltimore, Maryland 21211

Milliken, 1100 Research Boulevard, St. Louis, Missouri 63132

Milton Bradley Company, Springfield, Massachusetts 01101

Reader's Digest Services, Educational Division, Pleasantville, New York 10570

Skillcorp Software, 1711 McGraw Avenue, Irvine, California 92714

Society for Visual Education, 1345 Diversey Parkway, Chicago, Illinois 60614

Consumer information. These guidelines can help one who is purchasing instructional software to select programs that provide students with effective reinforcement for correct answers:

1 Feedback should be clear and intelligible to the user. This includes appropriate reading level if the reinforcement is in the form of a written message.

2 Reinforcers are most effective if they are delivered immediately after an answer is entered.

3 The pace of the reinforcement program should hold the user's interest. Lengthy animations or messages may not promote on-task behavior.

4 Personalized feedback that displays the user's name may be attractive to students.

5 Variety of feedback formats may be an important feature. Feedback can be more fun when it is unpredictable.

6 A gamelike format that delivers positive events after correct answers may motivate students to spend time at drill and practice.

Feedback After Errors

Appeal of feedback. Self-correcting feedback should be a clue to the learner, not a punishment. If the user receives an aversive sound or a demeaning message after entering an incorrect response, motivation may decrease. Teachers would cringe if an instructor said, "No, dummy!" to a student who made a mistake, yet some educational software delivers feedback with similarly unflattering language. Some software with audio gives a "raspberry" sound that is less than pleasant. The sound announces to the entire classroom that the person at the computer has made an error.

Instructional software can deliver feedback after an error in a nonaversive way. Written messages should avoid negative emotion. "Try again, Suzanne," "Here's a clue . . . ," and "You're close, Brad" are relatively unemotional statements that tell the student he has made an error. Language may be eliminated altogether, and the item, question, or problem may simply be presented again. Some programs answer an incorrect response with a flashing cursor and the chance to try another response. More sophisticated programming provides clues or complete tutorials after the student makes an error.

Multiple opportunities. It is sometimes beneficial to have instructional software allow the user more than one opportunity to enter a correct answer, except with true/false and multiple-choice formats. If entering a correct second answer depends more on chance than skill, then presenting the same item again after an error will not be very instructional. It is possible to program the content of a missed item to appear again in an item that looks different. For example, if the learner enters "false" in response to the statement, "A peninsula is a finger of land that is surrounded by a body of water," the program can provide another opportunity with the same content, such as "Florida is surrounded by water on three sides and is called a peninsula."

If the program provides the student with multiple opportunities to select a correct answer, there should be a point at which the program progresses. Some poorly designed instructional software traps students in a lesson if they are unable to enter a correct response. Nearly every piece of software can be exited by pressing a BREAK or RESET button, but well-designed programs do not require users to use such drastic and futile measures.

Provision of correct answers and cues. Constructive and instructive feedback after errors helps the student learn the right answer or correct problem-solving process. Software that allows the student to discover correct answers after entering an error helps make the student self-sufficient when working at the computer. A series of cues before the entire answer is given can require the learner to proceed through a structured problem-solving sequence. This type of practice in structured approaches to solving problems can be valuable for students with learning problems. Complex programming is required to achieve feedback with cues, and software of this level of sophistication may be more expensive than software that features a routine presentation of drill and practice.

Branching to tutorials. Programmers can design a "branching" feature in software that gives learners a tutorial lesson relating to the item on which an error was committed. The lesson may explain a process, restate an important rule, or break down the steps required to solve the problem. Tutorials may be brief examples or rather lengthy lessons. Ideally, the tutorials are appropriate for the type of error the student committed. Sophisticated error analysis and instructional design can make branching to tutorials an effective feature in educational software. If the tutorial lesson is lengthy and does not address the student's problem with the items, the student may consider the lesson a waste of time. The tutorial lesson should provide the correct answer eventually and allow the student to practice the correct response.

Opportunity for practice. After a learner has been provided with the correct answer or a tutorial, he should be required to practice entering the correct answer. A program that merely flashes the right answer and quickly proceeds to the next item does not ensure that the learner can actually achieve a correct answer. If the user has to perform the item successfully, and then is positively reinforced for the correct answer, chances are he will be able to repeat the correct performance in the future. Again, some mechanism should prevent the user's being trapped if he enters an incorrect answer repeatedly. Ideally, the program would route the user to a prerequisite task or tell the student to alert the teacher.

Examples of software that deliver corrective feedback. It is possible to find instructional computer programs that give the learner feedback after an error is entered. Hartley Courseware publishes a beginning reading program, "The Vowels Tutorial," that branches to a tutorial using a different word with the same vowel pattern. The student is required to apply a pattern and enter responses during the tutorial lesson. Love Publishing Company's "Software for Basic Math Skills" gives the learner multiple opportunities to arrive at a correct answer with the message, "Try again." If a second error is made, the screen says, "Let me show you," and the correct solution is worked on the screen. This program also delivers reinforcement for correct responses with visual and audio rewards.

Several microcomputer programs published by Media Materials allow the student multiple opportunities and then present the right answer on the screen along with the wrong answer to clarify understanding. The program then proceeds, never permitting the student to get stuck in the lesson. The "Assisted Instructional Development System" (A.I.D.S.), published by Skillcorp Software, allows content and format flexibility. The system is a program "shell" that structures computerized lessons according to the teacher's input. The lessons may provide structured hints and branching to enrichment, reinforcement, or remedial levels. Items may appear as multiple choice, true/false, matching, numeric ranges, or short answer. The system also features daily and cumulative student reports. A.I.D.S. is a relatively expensive piece of computer software.

The program entitled "Whole Number Arithmetic Series by Teaching Objective," published by the Society for Visual Education, features an error analysis at the end of the lesson. Student and teacher can see both the number and type of errors the student made during the lesson. In addition, the program tells how many times the student asked for help during the lesson. Software that keeps records is convenient for the teacher. Each student's work may be reviewed during planning time or at the teacher's convenience. Records that provide information about types of errors are more helpful than a percent-correct score. If the teacher has access to a printer, and the software permits, a printed copy is sometimes useful.

Consumer information. Instructional computer software can deliver feedback after the learner enters an incorrect response. These factors should be considered in evaluating instructional computer feedback after a learner enters an error:

1 Feedback should be appealing, unemotional, and quiet, rather than aversive sounds and negative statements.

2 Learners should have multiple opportunities to try to give the correct answer. A second or third try may be helpful, but not if chance becomes a greater factor than skill (for example, on the multiple-choice format).

3 Programs should not trap the student if he enters wrong answers repeatedly. The lesson should proceed in some fashion after the student makes a limited number of attempts.

4 After entering an error, students will find it helpful to have the correct answer displayed at some point in the lesson.

5 A series of cues can help the learner discover the correct answer to a problem on which an error was committed.

6 Sophisticated software branches the user to a tutorial lesson to learn how to make a correct response.

7 Students should have the opportunity to practice a correct response before the lesson proceeds to new items.

Selective Software Shopping

Microcomputer software for the classroom can be a major part of a materials budget. Costs for single programs range from twenty dollars to hundreds of dollars. Educators should select wisely both to benefit students and to reinforce publishers for quality programming. The amount of instructional computer software available is rapidly increasing, but the discriminating buyer will discover that only a portion of the software is well-designed.

Educational software has been criticized in the professional literature. Doig (1983) considers most current software for the classroom as "long on fun and short on learning" (p. 23). Some instructional programs are of inferior quality, and Hofmeister (1982) points out that much of it is unvalidated for use in the classroom. Apparently, many computer programmers are not teachers, and many teachers are not computer programmers. As communication improves among teachers and programmers, instructional software may improve. Until then, Budoff and Hutton (1982) recommend that teachers be aware of the "hype" about computers and establish criteria for acceptable software for their students.

Finding Software

Many of the larger educational materials publishers feature computer software. Teachers may already be receiving catalogs advertising microcomputer instructional programs. (See Table 10.2 for key phrases from educational catalogs that may indicate

Table 10.2   *Key phrases from educational materials catalogs that may indicate a self-correction feature*

"Correct answers provided"

"Branching"

"Allows students to progress only when the correct response is given"

"Provides immediate feedback"

"A breakdown of results after each session lets the student see exactly where strengths and weaknesses lie."

"Self-checking"

"If the answer is incorrect, it is followed by a sentence using the word in context. After a second incorrect response, the correct answer is displayed."

"Computer not only says if an answer is right or wrong, but provides the applicable rule for the correction"

"When an error is made, the student is taught the proper method of obtaining the correct answer."

"Helps a student understand why certain answers are correct and why other options are incorrect"

"Feedback on rules"

"Correct responses win students playing time on a special reward game."

"Only one try per problem—computer corrects mistakes immediately."

"If the student makes an error, the program branches to a brief tutorial."

"Computer stores any errors for future review."

"Visual and audio rewards for success with each problem"

"Students receive immediate reward or instruction."

"Students have access to a 'help' option whenever an incorrect response is entered."

a self-correcting feature.) State-approved vendors lists may be another starting place. Publishers' exhibits at conferences provide opportunities to make hands-on evaluations of software. Teachers and purchasers may be able to contact vendors who will make a classroom presentation, especially if a group of teachers is interested.

Computer education publications (see Table 10.3) not only advertise instructional software but sometimes also feature critical reviews of programs. In some areas, electronic bulletin board services are available to educators. The state department of education or local district computer consultant should know about such networks.

Another source of instructional software is teacher programming. Relatively sophisticated programs are possible with even beginning programming skills. The computer language BASIC is easy to learn and allows the teacher to include features such as personalized reinforcement, cues, corrective feedback, and multiple opportunities.

Funding Sources

In addition to an allotted classroom or program budget, alternative funding sources are available for software purchases.

Table 10.3 *Educational journals and magazines with information about computer software*

Review Journals
Dvorak's Software Review
The Journal of Courseware Review
MicroSIFT
Pipeline
Purser's Magazine
School Microwave Reviews
Software Review

Educational Computing Journals
Classroom Computer News
Educational Computer
Electronic Education
Electronic Learning
Microcomputers in Education
Micro-Scope
The Computing Teacher

Since computer technology and classroom applications are relatively new, research grants are available. Interested persons should consult government publications, university research offices, and publishers involved in educational computer materials. Some schools have acquired computers and computer software through service projects and sponsorship by community organizations.

Inspecting Software

Vendor demonstrations and conference exhibits allow teachers to work with software as a student would. In addition, some publishers will send samples or entire programs on approval. When a teacher inspects software, he should enter both correct and incorrect answers to check for reinforcement and corrective feedback. Other features to look for include multiple opportunities, practice entering a correct response, and tutorials.

Guarantees are important since software can be easily damaged during shipping or may not live up to its advertising. The following guarantee would be considered fairly typical: "If you are not completely satisfied with the software, return it to the company for a full refund or credit against purchase within 15 days of receipt. This policy does not apply to merchandise that has been abused or damaged in any way, and the company will not be liable for any incidental or consequential damages resulting from such defect."

Other Consumer Information

In addition to the factors pertaining to reinforcement and feedback, the consumer should be aware of several other points when purchasing instructional computer software.

1 Machine compatibility is important because many microcomputers use different computer languages. For instance, software written for one computer may not run on another computer.

2 The scope of the program's academic content should be evaluated against the price of the software. If one program provides only prac-

tice in addition of whole numbers, another program that also includes decimals and fractions at the same price may be a better buy.

3   A pretest/posttest within the program will help the teacher determine if the software is appropriate for individual students and if the content is mastered.

4   Visual appeal is an important factor in motivation. Avoid software that is difficult to read or has a boring screen display. The amount of text on the screen influences readability.

5   Instructional programs may either be machine-paced or self-paced. If the teacher intends for the student to work through material at his own rate, then a self-paced program is best. Under some circumstances, the teacher may prefer a machine-paced presentation. For the teacher who wishes to encourage increased speed in entering responses, some programs permit different rates of presentation.

6   Instructional software requires a wide range of keyboard skills. Learners may have to press RETURN, or they may have to enter long strings of words. The teacher may have to supervise a student's first trial with a piece of software to determine if keyboard skills are appropriate.

Summary

Computer software can deliver reinforcement and feedback in a variety of ways. If students use software featuring self-correction, they will probably make better use of time spent receiving instruction from the computer. Well-designed educational software encourages future correct responses. It also teaches a student why an error is wrong and what to do differently the next time. Teachers should select computer software that is more than an electronic workbook. The discriminating software consumer will demand microcomputer programs that apply proven principles of learning, including self-correction.

References

Budoff, M., and L. R. Hutton. "Microcomputers in Special Education: Promises and Pitfalls." *Exceptional Children, 49* (1982): 123–28.

Doig, S. K. "Feds Fund Efforts to Solve Software Drought." *Electronic Education, 2* (1983): 23–24.

Hofmeister, A. M. "Microcomputers in Perspective." *Exceptional Children, 49* (1982): 115–21.

Lathrop, A. "Microcomputer Software for Instructional Use: Where are the Critical Reviews?" *The Computing Teacher, 9* (1982): 22–26.

Computer Terms: A Glossary for the Classroom

People who work with computers have developed a jargon that can be confusing for those new to the field. This glossary includes terms that teachers and students will find helpful when using microcomputers in the classroom. Because it is sometimes difficult to discuss computers without using the jargon, some definitions contain other terms from the glossary. When a word in a definition is also an entry in the glossary, it is italicized.

Alphanumeric   All the letters, numbers, and symbols on a computer keyboard. If directions specify entry of an alphanumeric, any graphic symbol on the keyboard will be a correct response. Alphanumerics do not include keys such as BREAK, SHIFT, or CLEAR, as these keys do not cause the appearance of a symbol on the screen.

Backup   A copy of a computer *program.* Many commercially published pieces of *software* allow the *user* to make a limited number of copies, or backups, on a *disc* or cassette tape. Teachers often use the backups first and save the original. (It is a violation of copyright law to make unauthorized backups.)

BASIC   Acronym for Beginners All-Purpose Symbolic Instruction Code. BASIC is a computer *language* that features commands made up of simple English words and mathematical symbols. It is relatively easy to learn, and most brands of *microcomputers* can run *software* programmed in BASIC. There are several different versions of BASIC, and the version must be *compatible* with the brand of computer. For example, *programs* written in BASIC for use with one computer may not run on another computer.

Branching   A feature in a computer *program* that allows the *user* to receive an auxiliary program and then return to the main program. For example: the learner enters an incorrect response, automatically receives a short tutorial on that item, and then is returned to the regular sequence of the program. Branching is an effective tool for providing individualized practice and feedback.

Bug   Something that causes a *program* to run incorrectly or not at all. A bug may be due to a malfunction in the machine, a faulty connection between the computer and a *peripheral,* or an error in the computer program. To "debug" means to correct the problem.

Cathode Ray Tube (CRT) Television screen used for display purposes with a computer. Full capability for color *graphics* is desirable but expensive. Black-and-white CRTs adequately display most instructional *software.*

Coding Writing a computer *program.* This process often begins with a flow chart before commands are sequenced. Some programmers write the commands on paper as a step in coding; others code directly on the computer.

Compatibility All parts of the computer system *(hardware, software,* and *peripherals)* working together. Because computers developed very quickly in a competitive market, hardware, software, and peripherals are not all interchangeable. Those buying computer products must keep compatibility in mind.

Computer Assisted Instruction (CAI) *Software* designed to provide learners with instruction. CAI comes in a variety of forms, including drill and practice, tutorials, educational games, and *simulations.*

Computer Managed Instruction (CMI) *Software* designed to manage data in the classroom. Teachers use CMI to record, store, and get statistics on pretests, posttests, demographic information, daily rates, etc. CMI can reduce the amount of time it takes to keep good class records.

Courseware Instructional system including the computer *programs* and supporting materials such as books, worksheets, and teacher's manual.

Cursor Flashing marker indicating where on the screen the next character will appear. Usually when the cursor is present, the *program* is waiting for the *user* to type something. When the cursor is not present, the computer is generally busy executing a program.

Disc (also **Disk**) Flat, circular piece of material used to store computer *programs* and data. Some *microcomputers* use floppy discs; others use cassette tapes for the same purpose. Discs have the advantage of rapid access to information and commands.

Disc Drive The part of the computer system that interprets magnetic impulses from a *disc.* Some systems have more than one disc drive, which can simplify making *backups,* saving data in files, copying original programs, etc.

Disc Operating System (DOS) Set of *programs* that tell the computer how to perform basic computing functions. Most *software* will automatically load a DOS; some require that a DOS be loaded into the memory before the program will run.

Graphics Shapes and figures programmed to appear on a screen or printed page. *Microcomputers* can display two types of graphics: low and high resolution graphics. Low resolution graphics are easy to program, but do not have the detail of high resolution graphics. Graphics can be animated and can feature a range of colors.

Hardware The *computer* machine. Hardware includes the *processor,* keyboard, *disc drive(s),* cassette player, *joystick,* and printer. Hardware components can be purchased separately, but must be *compatible.*

Joystick Device that controls movement of the *cursor* or an image on the screen. Joysticks are most often used in playing games and are usually sticks or knobs that can be moved up, down, right, and left.

K Measure of the computer *hardware*'s storage capacity. Complex *programs* may require hardware with a large number of K. It is possible to expand the storage capacity of some systems beyond the original K value.

Language Specific set of commands used by a programmer to instruct the computer to perform specific actions. Computer languages are designed for various purposes. *BASIC* was originally designed to fit the needs of college students but has a wider use today. Some other computer languages are *Logo,* Pascal, and FORTRAN.

Logo Computer *language* designed to help young children learn about geometry, computer *graphics,* and basic computer programming.

Microcomputer Computer system that can run one *program* at a time. Microcomputers fit on a desk top and are sometimes called "personal computers."

Peripheral Accessory that can be attached to the computer *processor.* Peripherals include printers, *disc drives,* separate keyboards, *joysticks,* and cassette players.

Processor That part of the computer system that does the work. A processor receives commands and executes them. The processor in a *microcomputer* is made up of tiny silicon chips.

Program Series of commands written in a computer *language* that causes the computer to perform.

Simulation Computer *software* designed to guide the learner through a representation of a real or imaginary situation. Simulation software can provide practice in problem-solving situations that might otherwise be difficult to represent in the classroom.

Software Computer *programs* stored on *discs* or cassettes. The computer *hardware* reads the magnetic impulses on the software and executes directions contained in the program. Software from commercial publishers is copyrighted, but it is sometimes possible to make a limited number of *backup* discs or cassettes.

User Person at the computer keyboard who is entering responses or directions and interacting with the computer.